249

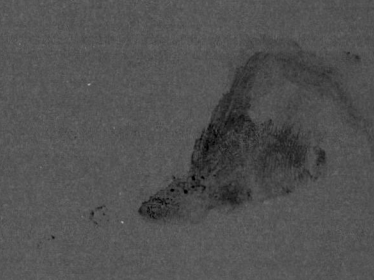

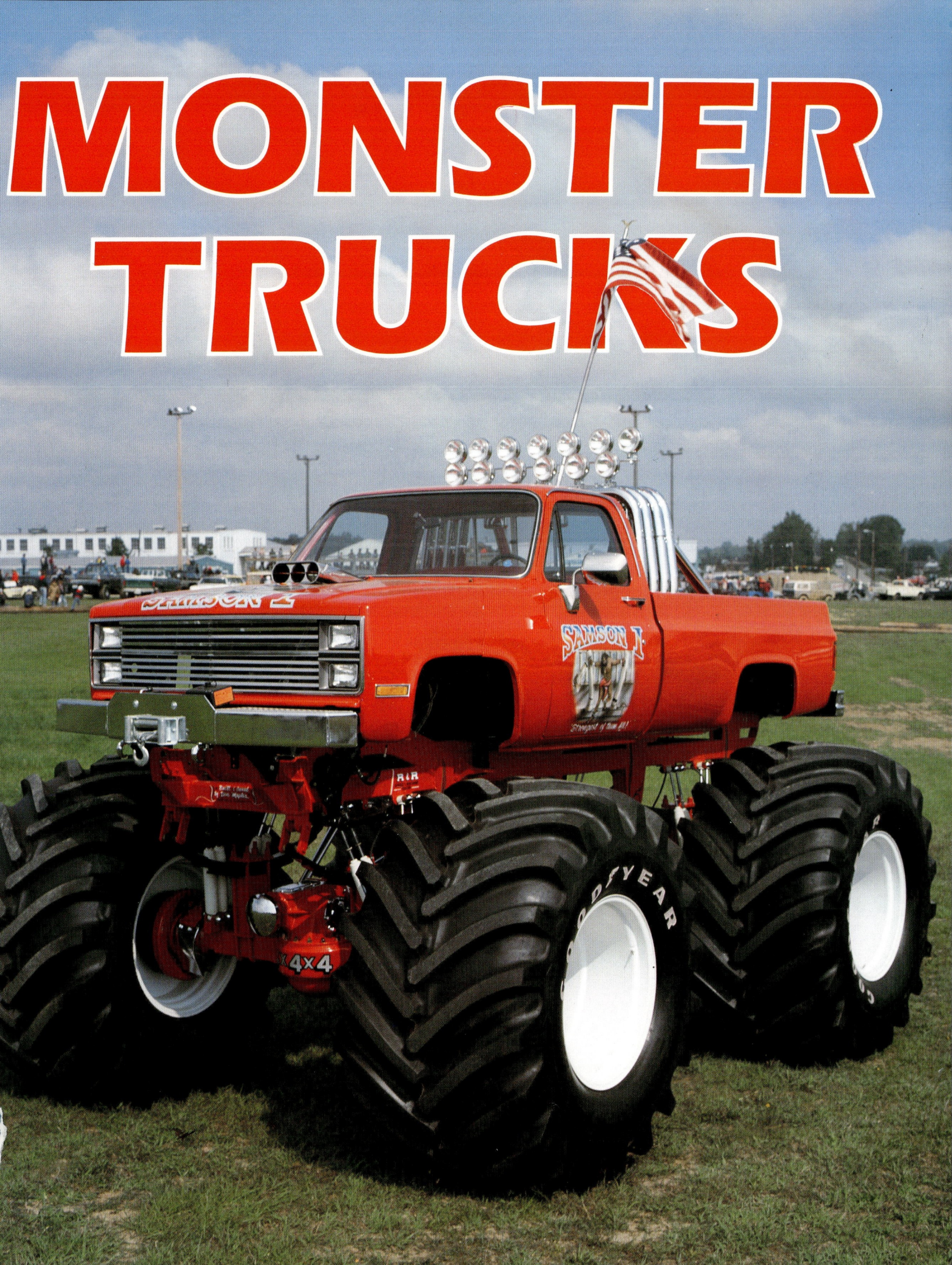

MONSTER TRUCKS

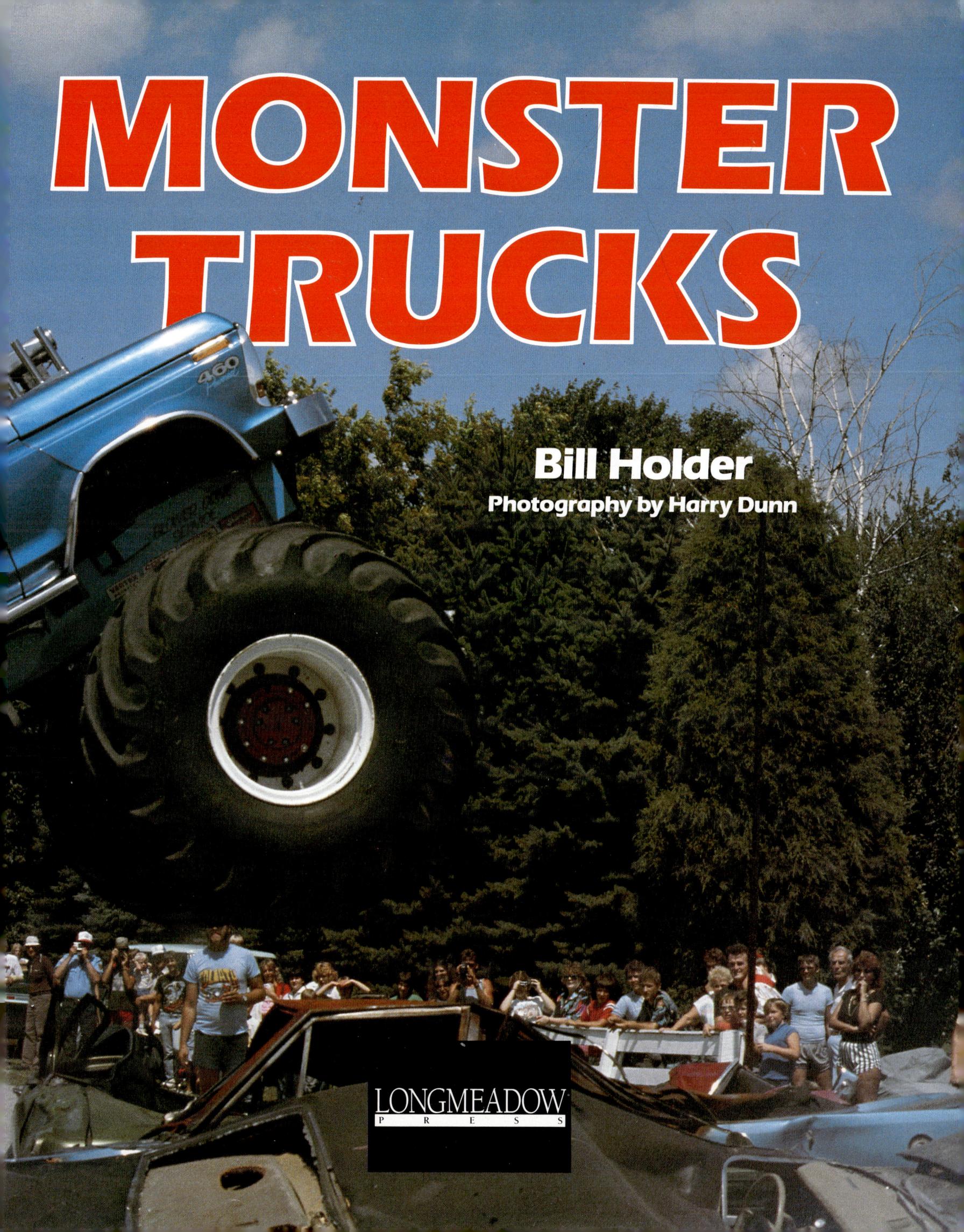

MONSTER TRUCKS

Bill Holder
Photography by Harry Dunn

LONGMEADOW
PRESS

All rights reserved. No part of this book may be reproduced or utilized in any form or by any means, electronic or mechanical, including photocopying, recording or by any information storage and retrieval system, without permission in writing from the copyright holder.

This 1992 edition published by
Longmeadow Press
201 High Ridge Road
Stamford CT 06904

Produced by
Brompton Books Corporation
15 Sherwood Place
Greenwich CT 06830

ISBN 0-681-41680-7

Printed in Hong Kong

0 9 8 7 6 5 4 3 2 1

Photography Assistance from David Tucker, Suzy Hall, Valeria and John D Farquhar.
Technical Assistance from Pulling Power Magazine.
Typing support from Gayle Sargent.
Edited by Glenn Holder.

Page 1: *Samson I* on display.

Pages 2-3: A car-crushing *Goliath* monster.

This page: A front view of *Thumper* shows its wide stance.

Contents

Here They Come	6
The Beginnings	8
What Makes These Things Go?	14
Point A to Point B	30
It's Showtime	36
Monsters in the Public Eye	52
Odd Balls	54
Monster Trucks Illustrated	60

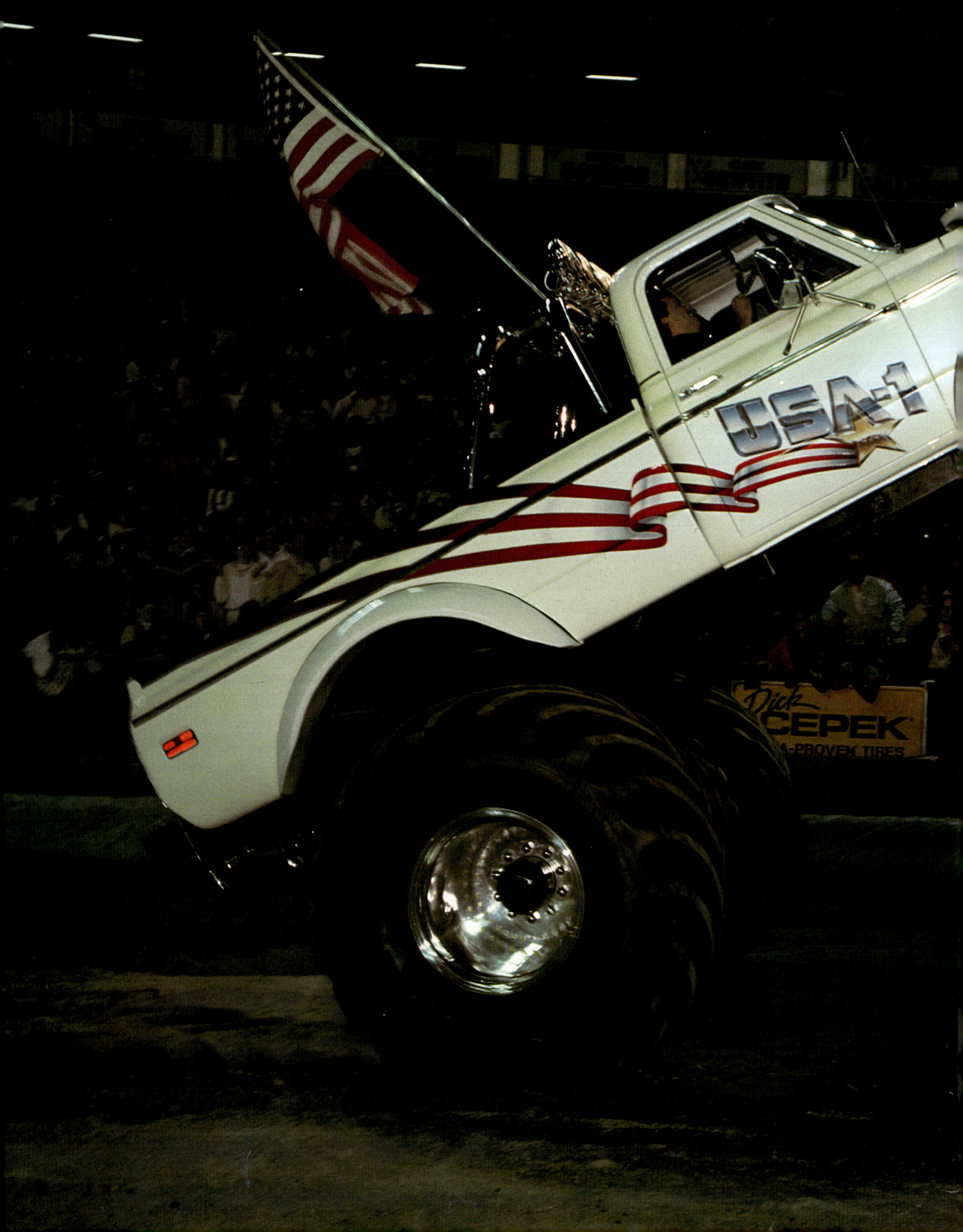
USA-1
Dick CEPEK

Here They Come

They come from the four corners of the world. In their path they leave heaping masses of twisted metal and shattered glass. There are giant footprints left where they have walked and the earth has huge scars that will withstand the passing of time. They belch fire and their voices crack the night air with a vengeance. They make a sound like none other known to mortal man. They come in waves, dozens and dozens of them in a procession of mass destruction. There's *Bigfoot* and *Goliath, Godzilla* and *Frankenstein, Hercules* and *Samson.* Nothing can stop their onslaught and no one dares try. No one dares stand in their way. These are the monster trucks—the most awesome vehicles ever to rumble over the earth's surface.

The term 'monster' really fits these huge four-wheel-drive vehicles. Be it their monstrous six-foot tires or their monstrous height and weight, they truly are monsters in every sense of the word.

First it was television, then came the hula hoop, followed closely by CB radios and music videos. Now, in the 1980s, it's monster trucks that have taken over the imagination and tantalized the senses. But are they just a passing fancy? Or are they part of a new generation that will survive, endure and flourish for decades to come? How did they get here and what makes them the phenomenon of the eighties? Why does every kid from eight to eighty have wild fantasies about owning, driving or merely riding in these 10-ton marvels of mechanical science?

The answers to these questions, and many more, are contained in the colorful chapters that follow. So, if the heart can take it, tighten the seat belt and explore the amazing world of monster trucks!

Maybe one of the most famous shots is this wheelstand photo of Everett Jasmer's *USA-1* Chevy. This was one of the first wheelstands done in front of a big crowd.

The Beginnings

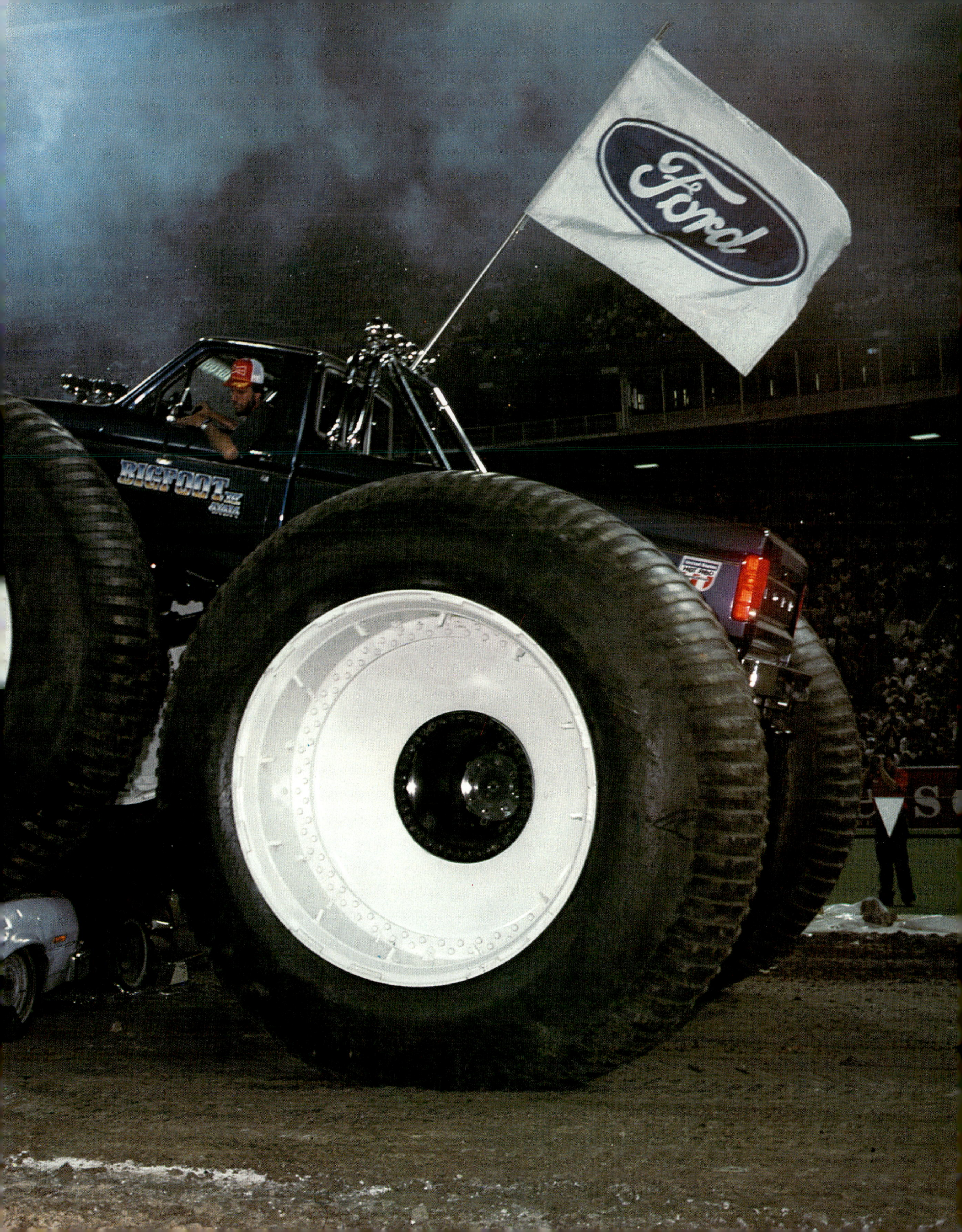
Ford
BIGFOOT

Pages 8-9: Attention to detail is a watchword for *Bigfoot*. Notice the Ford flag, a major *Bigfoot* sponsor.

Above: A complete line of *Bigfoot* merchandise is carried to all Bigfoot events.

Right: Bob Chandler is always available for a photo or for conversation with curious fans.

To understand the origins of the monster truck, there must first be an understanding of the four-wheel-drive (4WD) industry some 12 years ago. The mid-seventies were a time when America's major auto-makers were reeling in the wake of a gas crunch. Long gas lines and even-odd rationing systems were the major topics of conversation, taking up all the primetime television news broadcasts and making headlines in America's newspapers. Gas had taken on the same importance as gold bullion.

What this shortage did was awaken a sleeping public to the fact that the country was driving a huge fleet of oversized gas guzzlers. No one knew that more, or soon would suffer from it more, than the GM, Ford and Chrysler companies. Then, when the flow of gas was restored to almost normal, a tidal wave of reaction came from the American car-buying public. Small, fuel-efficient cars became the in thing to own and the influx of small foreign cars capitalized on the situation.

For the first time, America also became aware that it was possible to have a vehicle that was both fun and functional, kind of a one-size-fits-all type of vehicle. What better than a 4WD truck? Quickly the Big Three auto-makers pumped out 4WD's and the public started to snatch them up. Small or large, it didn't make any difference. Americans wanted 4WD trucks.

From this rush for the 4WD vehicles blossomed the inevitable. The love of leisure-time activities was no stranger to the younger set who now opted for the Ford F series or a Dodge Red Ram rather than a Ford LTD or a

The Beginnings 11

12 Monster Trucks

Left: *Ms Bigfoot* is built on a Ford Ranger theme and has drawn as much attention because of it as have the other trucks.

Below: The most unique addition to the *Bigfoot* stable was *Ms Bigfoot*, which is, of course, driven by a lady.

The Beginnings

Pontaic Bonneville. Four-wheel-drive clubs sprang up like flowers in May. Magazines devoted to the industry, which had been around but with limited success, now flourished. Club outings became 'happenings' rather than just get-togethers and all eyes were on this rapidly-growing division of the automotive industry.

One of those dyed-in-the-wool four-wheelers was Bob Chandler of Hazelwood, Missouri. The middle-aged Chandler had been dabbling in the world of 4WD's since he and his wife Marilyn first bought a truck for fun in the late 1960's. A man with great foresight, Bob saw the handwriting on the wall long before most, and he and a few friends unceremoniously opened a small 4WD shop in Hazelwood.

'I knew that advertising our shop was going to be the key to success for us,' Chandler remembers today. 'The only problem was we didn't have a lot of extra money to put out for magazine, radio or TV ads. So instead we would take my Ford truck and do various things to it with the products and services that we sold at the store. I'd go to the various 4WD truck-ins, as they called them, and people would ask me where I got this part or who put that on for me. It worked great.'

The trial-and-error method of testing new parts and 4WD accessories led Chandler and crew into bizarre experiments with old military equipment, such as rear ends and other related running gear. What was installed on Monday was then torn out the following Sunday. On returning to the shop Bob's shop foreman, Ron Magruder, would chastise Chandler for destroying all those freshly-installed parts. He teased that Bob had a big foot that was always planted flat on the accelerator pedal. The name stuck, and thus the famous epithet *Bigfoot* was born.

From there, Bob took a firm grip on what he could see as an aspiring new entity. His out-of-proportion truck became the talk of the 4WD world. 'Have you seen *Bigfoot*?' became the most frequently-asked question at all the off-road events, club picnics, mud racing meets and anywhere else there were more than two 4WD aficionados. Pardon the pun, but Bob Chandler had created a monster.

Almost simultaneously to Chandler there were others with the same idea. The main difference, though, was that the Missouri native was months ahead of the fast closing pack. A small touch of irony to the story is that Bob helped his soon-to-be-rivals in the construction of their trucks. Men like Fred Shafer and Jack Willman (*Bearfoot*), Jeff Dane (*King Kong*) and Everett Jasmer (*USA-1*) were hot on Chandler's heels with monster trucks of their own.

All this took place in the mid-to-late 1970's. These men and their trucks were the forerunners of today's growing list of monster trucks. They can best be compared to the pioneers of our American West. Bob Chandler was the 'scout' who searched for new territory. He was followed by the 'settlers' Dane, Jasmer, Shafer and Willman. The ranks have swollen to huge 'wagon train' numbers today.

As time has passed more and more men have entered the scene of the monster truck. To date there are approximately 140 to 150 of the creations around and the number grows almost weekly. The reason for the abundance of vehicles is fairly clear. As their popularity has grown, so has the need for more vehicles. The law of supply and demand takes over.

Their history has been very easy to trace. One need look no further than Hazelwood, Missouri to find its roots. The branches of the tree are everywhere.

What Makes These Things Go?

Above: Chrome literally covers the powerplant of the *Bearfoot* truck.

Right: Ford power is abundant on the *Virginia Giant*.

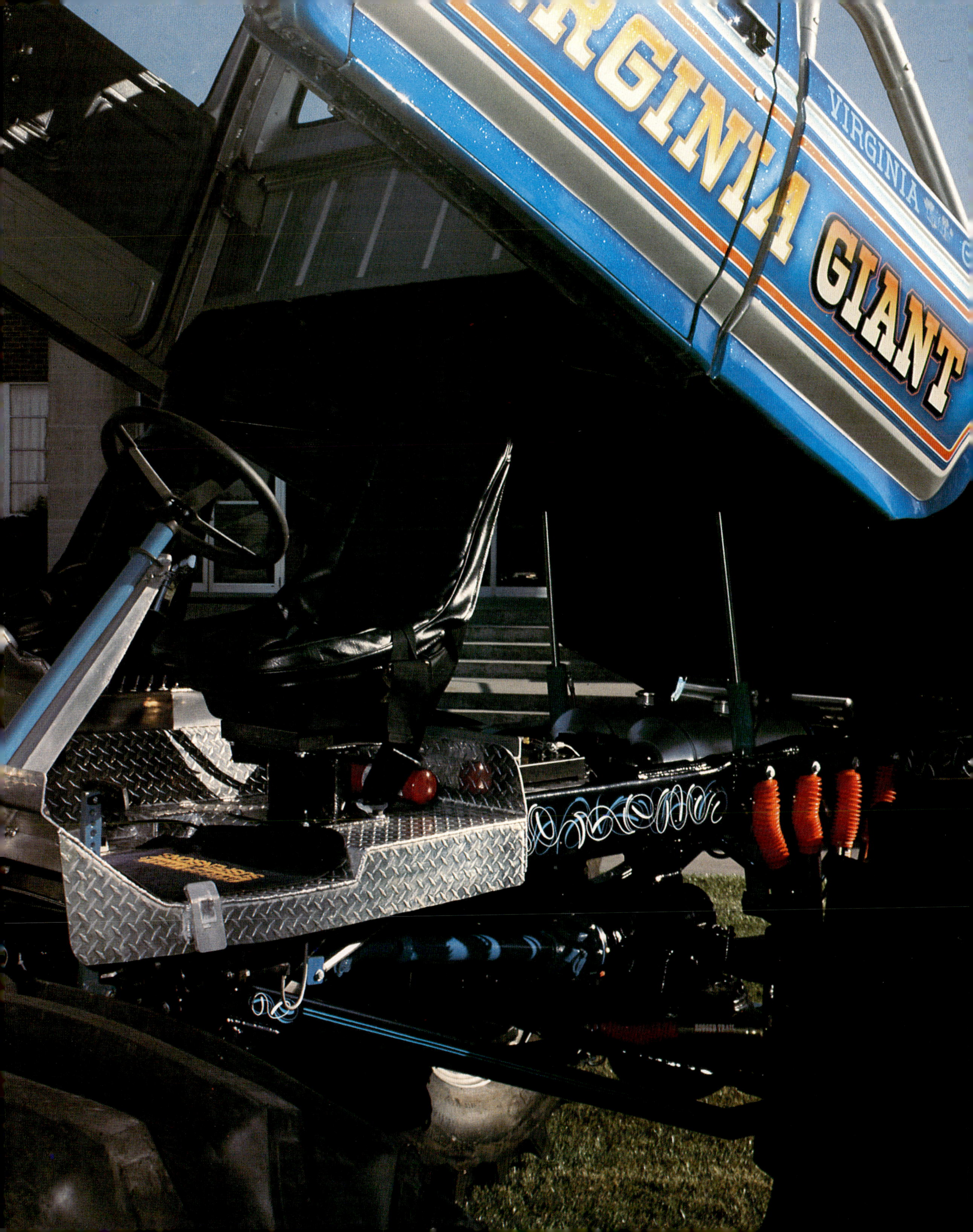
GIANT
VIRGINIA

Monster Trucks

The tall trucks, when you really get down to it, are still nothing more than four-wheel-drive pickup trucks. The same components that are required to drive the wheels of a Chevy or a Ford pickup are also required for the monster trucks.

But there are obviously some big differences between the short and the tall trucks. The job of turning these giant wheels alone is an awesome job. But add to that job the fact of having the monsters pull wheelies, power through giant lakes of mud, or blast their huge weights over cars or buses, and it's easy to see these giants are different beasts.

Power is required in huge levels of raw horsepower, and the powertrain components—namely the transmissions and axles—must be hand-built and of heavy duty construction. Many of the monster trucks, which can weigh up to 20,000 pounds, are pushing the vehicle strength requirements to their limits and beyond. There has actually been a new automotive science born to support these giant exhibition vehicles.

The construction of a monster truck begins with the frame. Many builders come up with their own ideas for building this integral part of the machine, but in all cases the criterion is the same—*to make it strong!* When you consider that the frame will have to support a vehicle weighing from seven to ten tons, it's easy to understand the importance of that ultimatum. Some builders start with

Top: Power to the rear wheels is provided by the driveshaft and the rear differential. Heavy-duty components are a definite necessity in these trucks.

Above: Close-up of the *Aces High* front differential and frame. Note the beautiful detailing on this monster truck.

Right: Tilt hoods have become commonplace in the tall trucks, as exhibited here by *Bearfoot*.

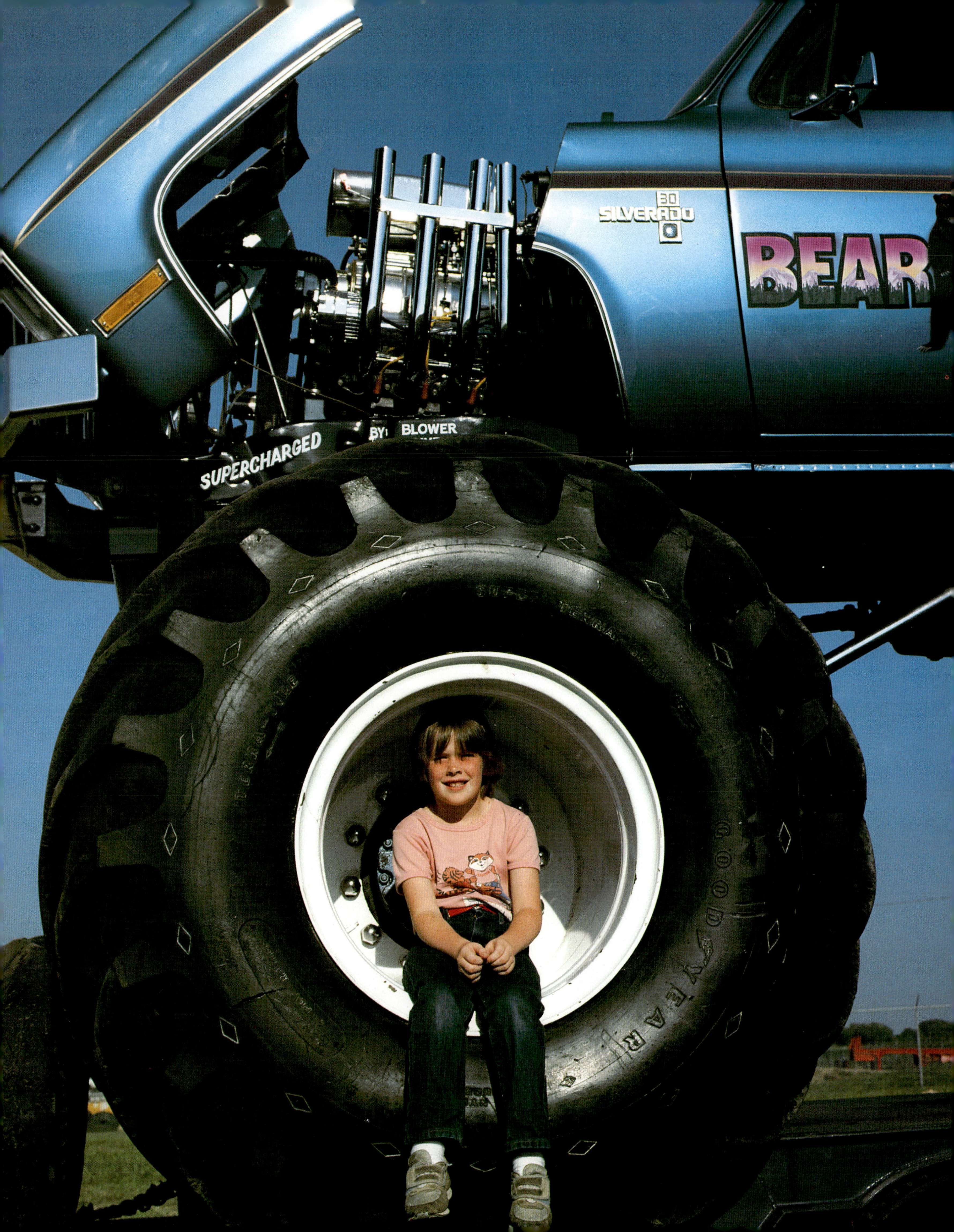
SILVERADO
30
BEAR
SUPERCHARGED
BY: BLOWER
GOODYEAR

18 Monster Trucks

ex-military frame hardware and then modify that hardware with their own bits and pieces. Such was the technique that was used by Cliff Starbird of Grand Rapids, Michigan on his *Monster Vette* monster truck. On the *Ice Monster Jr*, builder Brett Engelman started out with a new frame built out of three-by-six inch rectangular stock, and then literally set the original frame from his '78 Chevy-bodied vehicle on top of it. 'With the things that we are now doing with these trucks, you just have to make them super strong,' driver Jess Burgey of the *Ice Monster Jr* explained.

Kenny Fewox of the *Outlaw 35* monster truck of Polk City, Florida demonstrated several years ago why it's so important to have that frame strength. His red '35 Ford-based monster was actually the first tall truck to ever break in two. It happened in the New Orleans Superdome when the truck reared almost straight up, and then came down very hard with its thousands of pounds following it down.

Below: The gleaming front differential and frame of the *Aces High* monster truck.

Bottom: Shock absorbers in large numbers are a necessary part of every monster truck suspension system, as seen here on *Thumper*.

Right: A tilt hood is a necessity on any monster truck these days.

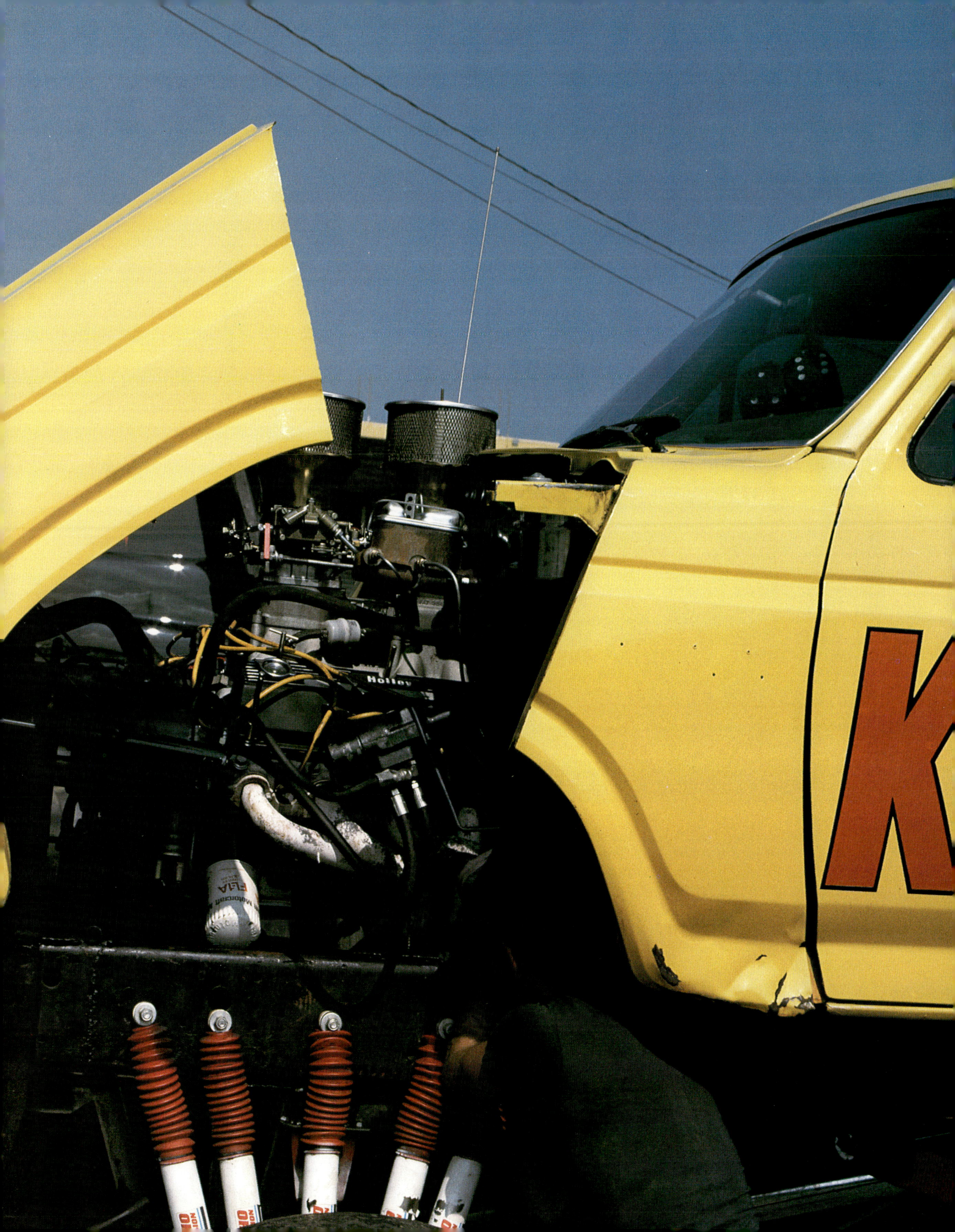
Holley

20 Monster Trucks

Below: The beefed-up suspension and heavy-duty shock absorbers of *Hercules*.

Right: In the *Virginia Giant*, the complete body tilts upward at the back.

A huge center beam serves as the main support for Larry Tura's *Hercules* monster truck of Clairton, Pennsylvania. In this interesting truck, the beam also serves as the pivot point for the whole body which Larry lifts, revolving around the rear of the truck.

Many monster trucks use so-called Ladder Bars which keep the springs from twisting. But before the monster trucks can do anything, there has to be that powerful motor under the hood. Just about every combination of motor components can be found in the growing number of big block Chevy or Ford motors. Almost all of the powerplants are more than 450 cubic inches of displacement. Many of them are bored out, adding another 50 or 75 additional inches. The *Samson I* of Don Maples has such a set-up in his truck with a 500 + cubic Chevy mill. It then carries a 6.71 supercharger which is actually overdriven by 12 percent. There are also two 75 Holley Carbs, a Competition Cam, and 12-1 TRW Pistons. 'It's well over 1000 horsepower,' Don explained.

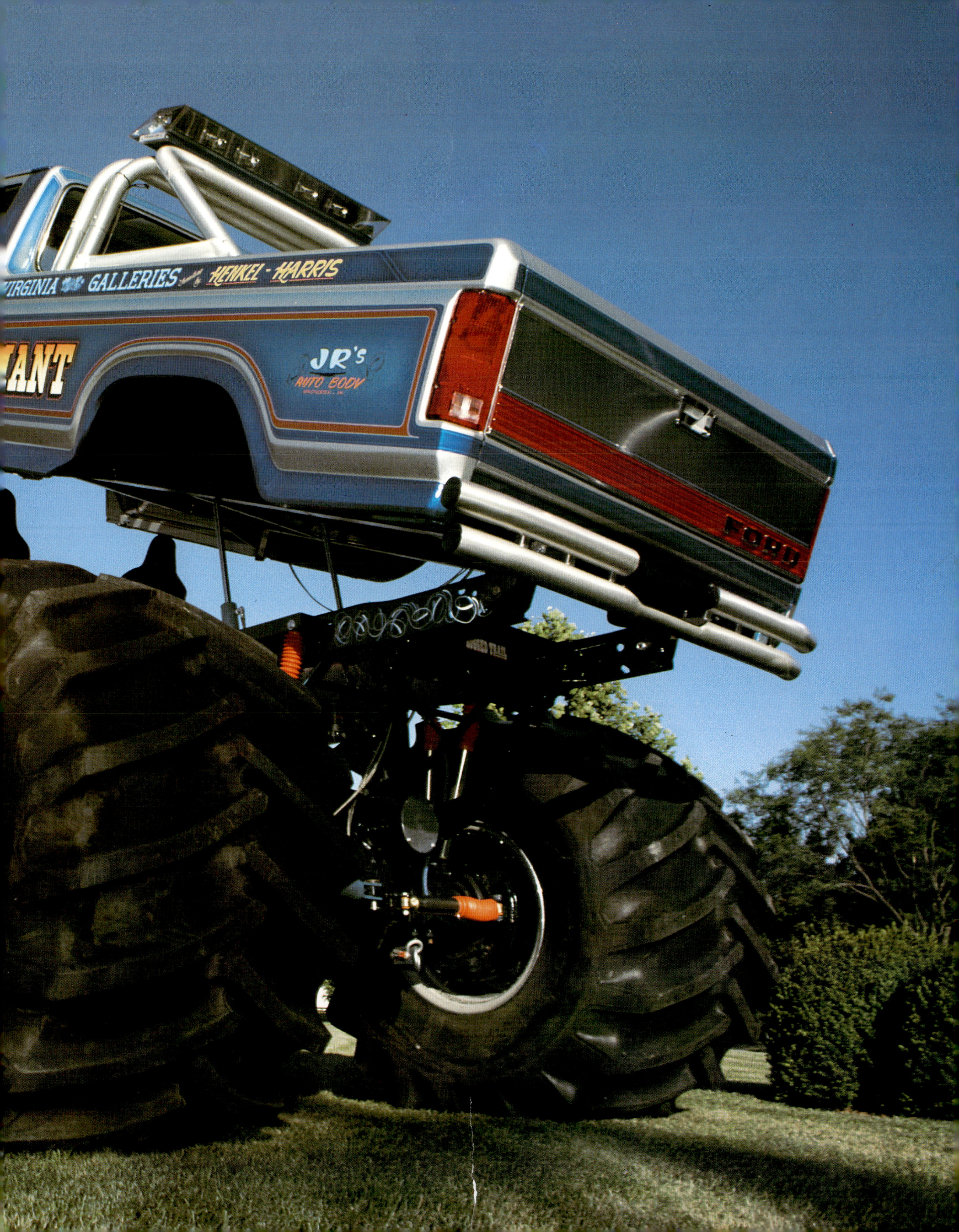
VIRGINIA GALLERIES
HENKEL - HARRIS
JR's
AUTO BODY
FORD

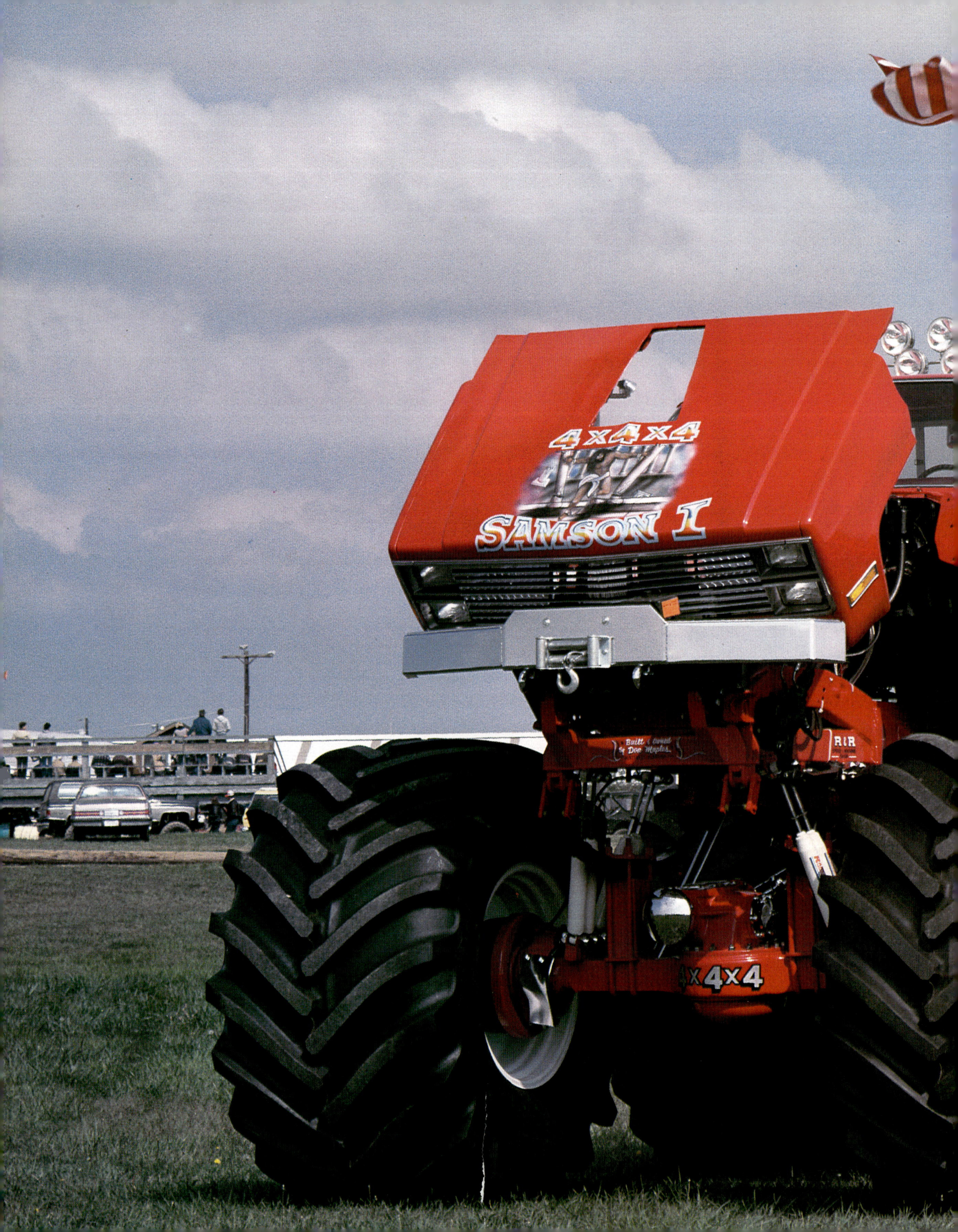

4x4x4
SAMSON I
4x4x4

Samson I displays its tilt hood.

Inset: A close-up of the *Virginia Giant's* powerful engine and suspension system.

The 460-cubic-inch Ford big blocks, though, are also excellent monster truck powerplants. The *Goliath* big wheeler uses such a set-up with a blower and considerable internal engine work. Of course, the *Bigfoot* monster is also the most famous user of FoMOCo power.

Not every tall truck uses the tremendous power boost provided by a supercharger. Several of the big machines kick up their horsepower figures with nitrous oxide systems. The nitrous system of Scott Stephens' *King Krunch* machine adds 200 horsepower to do its many jobs. Other trucks use the less powerful—but still quite effective—tunnel ram arrangement. Still others use just the standard carburation set-up, mostly with Predator Carbs.

24 Monster Trucks

Above: *Hercules* monster uses a 460 CID mill with two domination carbs and a tunnel ram set-up.

Right: *Thumper's* awesome rig is complete with tilt hood.

Some of the monster truck powerplants use alcohol fuel. There are several reasons for that choice. It produces more power, causes less engine wear, and it doesn't get as hot, all attributes that racecar mechanics have known for years.

The next link in the monster truck powertrains is pretty common in all trucks. They all use automatic transmissions—no stick shifts in these machines. The most popular trannies are the Ford C-6's and the General Motors Turbo 400's. Of course, many of the trucks have modified the transmissions, and strengthened them for their strange new jobs.

Following the transmission is the so-called transfer case where the power is split to proceed to the front and rear wheels. Gear reduction is also accomplished by this unit. There are some monster trucks that actually have two transfer cases. Such an arrangement is reportedly easier on the powertrain. The *Hercules* has so-called drop-boxes that drop the power from the transfer case to the rear ends without the steep angle.

What Makes These Things Go? 25

26 Monster Trucks

Then it's on to the front and rear differentials, or rear ends. When monster trucks first came on the scene, the standard units from four-wheel-drive trucks were used. No more. The units now sometimes come from five-ton military trucks, while other trucks use planetary rear ends, such as those used in tractors. The axles connecting all these components to drive the giant wheels often have the words 'US Government' etched into their metal. The *Bearfoot* truck has a pair of rear ends, one in the front and one in the rear, to help lessen the angle of the driveshaft.

The tires themselves also come in about as many sizes as do the monster trucks themselves. The most popular size with today's trucks, though, seems to be the 66-inch in diameter monsters, although there are a number of the 73-inch variety. But not surprisingly, *Bigfoot* has done them all one better as the magic of Bob Chandler carries a set of unbelievable ten-feet winter tundra tires for some of the truck's peculiar duties.

Holding the high-perched bodies stable is the job of some of the high-tech suspension systems. Since the trucks are sporting two to three foot lifts, a multitude of sturdy shocks per wheel helps stabilize things when the trucks come back down to Mother Earth. It also goes without saying that the springs in these trucks are extremely stiff and strong.

Steering is an important requirement for monster trucks to be able to do their thing. Many of the monster trucks

Thumper and *Godzilla* illustrate the unbelievably wide stance of the monster trucks.

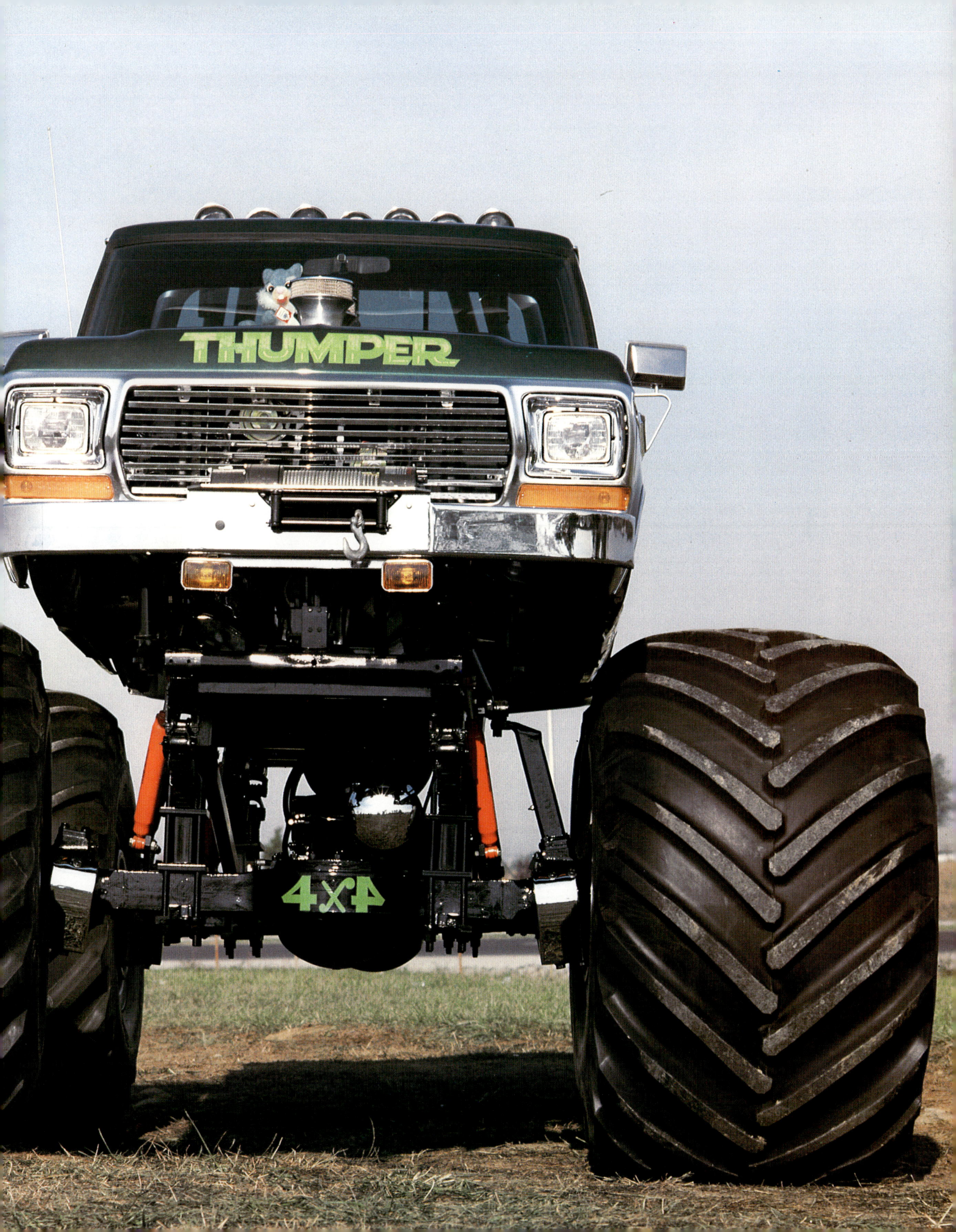
THUMPER
4X4

have independent steering on both front and rear. It enables some of the trucks to actually turn within their own length. It's quite a sight to see one of these trucks coming straight at you with the body at a 45-degree angle.

Stopping a many-pound truck is a sizable job. Most of the trucks use large disc brakes on all four wheels. Some trucks also have a driveline brake, with which stopping pressure is applied directly to the driveline.

One of the straight steering set-ups is demonstrated by *Blue Thunder* truck which has a helicopter joy stick instead of a steering wheel in the driver's compartment. The buttons mounted on the stick control a number of other vehicle functions as well. The *Blue Thunder* is definitely a one-of-a-kind monster.

The bodies on top of these monster trucks are widely varied, to say the least, and not all are even trucks! New pickup trucks, old and older pickup trucks, new cars and old cars, vans and the many other vehicles have contributed their bodies to the cause. The bodies themselves serve as little more than an attraction to the fans in the stands.

Safety, though, is a serious consideration with these machines. The floors in the bodies have been beefed up considerably to protect the driver from any powertrain failure which might occur below him. There is also a hearty roll cage built within the body, or outside, to protect the driver should the unthinkable ever happen and the truck flip over on top of him. Also for safety purposes, there is a driveshaft loop to protect the driveshaft and a scattershield around the transmission. Finally, most monster trucks carry fire extinguishers.

Many monster trucks have the capability to hydraulically lift their bodies off the frame, while others demonstrate the lifting of the hood. The *Hercules* lifts its entire body up from the frame. Undoubtedly, something else—who knows what—will be attempted in the future. There's always something new in this business.

But the drivers of these trucks, which sometimes cost as much as a 100,000 dollars and more, also go for beauty. Polished chrome is everywhere on these machines, the wheels, the roll bars, and especially under the hood. The engines glisten in the sunlight, reflecting the many thousands of dollars the truckers have invested in those motors. The paint jobs are also show-stopping. Many coats of bright colors, fancy lettering and air-brushed murals are standard fare for the monsters.

Lighting is but another fascinating feature on these machines. Almost the whole fleet of tall trucks carries a row of strobe lights across the top of the cab, which hikes the total height of many of them up to 14 feet. *Goliath* has an amber marker light arrangement which circles the sides of the truck. The lights travel around the truck like a police scanner.

One thing is for sure with this strange fleet of trucks—there's no way to ever order one at the neighborhood truck dealership. No way, because each of these vehicles is a one of a kind!

What Makes These Things Go?   29

Far left top: The *Pac Man* monster advertises its trade.

Far left center: The *Outlaw 35* offers a flashy way to write its name.

Far left bottom: The *Godzilla* uses a dinosaur in its airbrushed graphics. The sketches cover the hood and sides of the truck.

Left: *Aces High* displays its slick graphics.

Bottom left: Heavy chrome and patriotic colors cover the *Virginia Beast*.

Below: The elaborate little *Bearfoot* drawing depicts the truck in the mountains with a bear.

Bottom: A dramatic paint job characterizes *Hercules*.

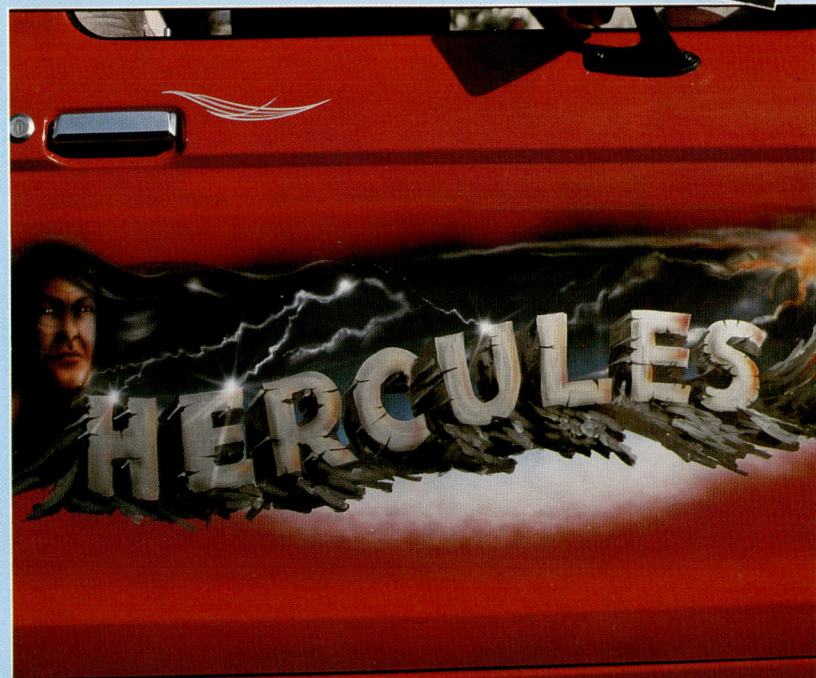

ERCULES
Ranger
VERTEX
MAGNETOS
CROWER
racing cams
Holley
PUMPS
trail master
trail master

Point A to Point B

Monster Trucks

A rosy picture may have been painted of the glamorous world of monster trucks, but there are two sides to owning a monster truck. Someone once said, 'All that glitters isn't gold,' and such is the case in the world of monster trucks. There are many dozens of monster trucks, cars, vans and other assorted vehicles, all vying for attention. However, the attention they are striving for most isn't with the fans—it's with the promoters.

The easiest comparison to use is the video cassette recorder. In the mid-seventies, when the first machine hit the American market, prices were out of sight. A machine could run as high as 1400 dollars and a bargain was anything under 1000. As more and more companies came into the fold, prices dropped significantly. Today the same machine that went for 1400 dollars goes for 300 dollars, and there isn't a waiting list to buy one either. The monster truck owners have suffered the same fate.

The first half dozen trucks built were extensions of an already-existing business. Bob Chandler *(Bigfoot)*, Jeff Dane *(King Kong)*, Everett Jasmer *(USA-1)* Fred Shafer and Jack Willman *(Bearfoot)* and Dave Spiker *(Eagle, Ms. All-American* and *All-American)* were then, as they are now, in the four-wheel-drive business. Each man owned and operated a business that hinged completely on the four-wheel-drive world. These monster trucks were as much of an advertisement for their business as magazine, television or radio ads would be. Their trucks represented their business enterprises. When these men started to reap the benefits of their labor and their creations became sensationally popular, others took notice. From then on, the push was on from every corner of the country to own 'your very own monster truck.'

As the demand was filled, the flooded market put the controls back into the hands of the promoters. The time when the truck owners could dictate their price was over, as the promoter could pick and choose from the growing list. Out and out bargaining by the monster truck owners drove the price down as each owner undercut his competitor to get that date. The very same scenario holds true today. The promoters, be it truck and tractor pull, mud bogging, custom car show or any other, realize they are in the driver's seat.

About the only salvation for some of the monster truck owners has been to land major sponsors, but even those opportunities are slim. Everett Jasmer *(USA-1)* has a good working agreement with True Value Hardware Company, as does *Bigfoot* with Ford Motor Company. Seth Doulton from Santa Barbara, California, has the US Tobacco Company, makers of Skoal and Copenhagen smokeless tobacco, as a major sponsor and his 1966 Chevy is lettered and painted in the company's green and white colors. As was mentioned elsewhere, toy companies have added to many of the monster truck drivers' coffers. Probably the most unique sponsor of any monster truck comes from the cold countryside of Minnesota where Milton Bell has a local church which backs his *Sons of Thunder II* Dodge. All proceeds from the truck go back to the church.

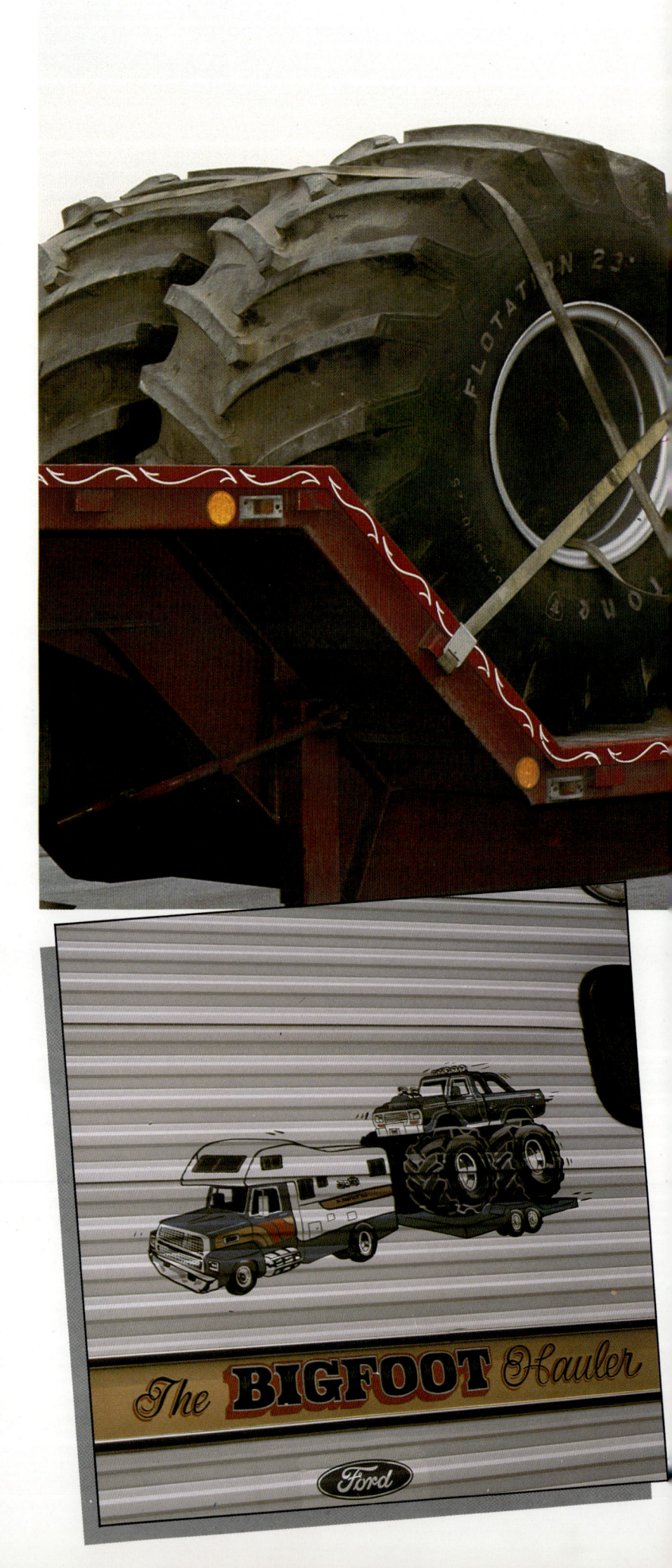

Point A to Point B   33

Pages 30-31: It's a huge job to load up *Hercules*, even with small wheels, along with securing the 66-inch tires.

Above: It's a long load when the *Hercules* monster truck and all its supporting equipment hit the road, which they do a lot.

Left: That famous *Bigfoot* name is shown on its hauler. Just the name says it all – nothing else is needed.

Right: Haulers are as good-looking as the trucks themselves. Here's the *USA-1* prime mover.

A novel approach for a sponsor is the one used for the *Virginia Giant* Ford, driven by Diehl Wilson and owned by Bill Henkel, both of Winchester, Virginia. Henkel owns one of the finest furniture companies in the country, and his 'Virginia Galleries' name and logo hold a prominent place on the multicolored Ford. The reason for building the truck? To advertise the company and do it in the same fashion as their furniture—first class.

Of the many monsters out there, only a handful have the type of sponsor that can really help defray the cost of the truck. After the initial expense of building the truck, it doesn't stop there. Getting the big truck to and from events creates a monumental problem in itself. One doesn't load up a seven-ton truck and all the extra needed goodies on a single-axle trailer and head off into the sunset. A flat-bed semi with a handful of highway permits and a big tank of fuel is more like what's required. Who said that 'getting there is half the fun?'

Think about the situation that Bob Chandler has at Bigfoot, Inc. Here's a guy with seven, count' em, seven trucks touring the four corners of America and overseas. That means he has seven teams that include driver, two or more crew members, merchandise and a big hauler that must accommodate all of the aforementioned items. What one has here is a logistical nightmare. But the savior to all this has been the computer system that the Bigfoot

Above: The precise operation of loading *Godzilla* on its hauler.

Right: The *Walkin' Tall* tall truck looks a bit strange standing in small travel tires.

Inc has in operation. All the necessary facts are fed daily into the computer, giving coordinators the 100 percent control needed to monitor an operation the size of Bigfoot.

The Bigfoot group, though, isn't the only computer-oriented monster truck team out there. Dave Spiker's Lakewood, Florida (*All-American, Eagle* and *Ms. All-American*) operation is just a keyboard away. Spiker's trucks can be located in a matter of minutes, and he can determine where they are scheduled for the next six months in the same amount of time. More and more monster truck owners are going the computer route.

This is not the easy life that many a paying spectator envisions as he sits eating his hot dog. Many miles add up to many more miles. Laws prohibiting the monster trucks from being hauled with their giant Goodyear tires mounted on the truck mean hours of back-breaking tire changes before and after each performance. And it always seems to rain or snow at just about that time. With all the financial and logistical considerations, with the promoters and sponsors, the teams and equipment, the world of monster trucks is certainly a complex one. There is much more to this exciting and glamorous domain than meets the eye.

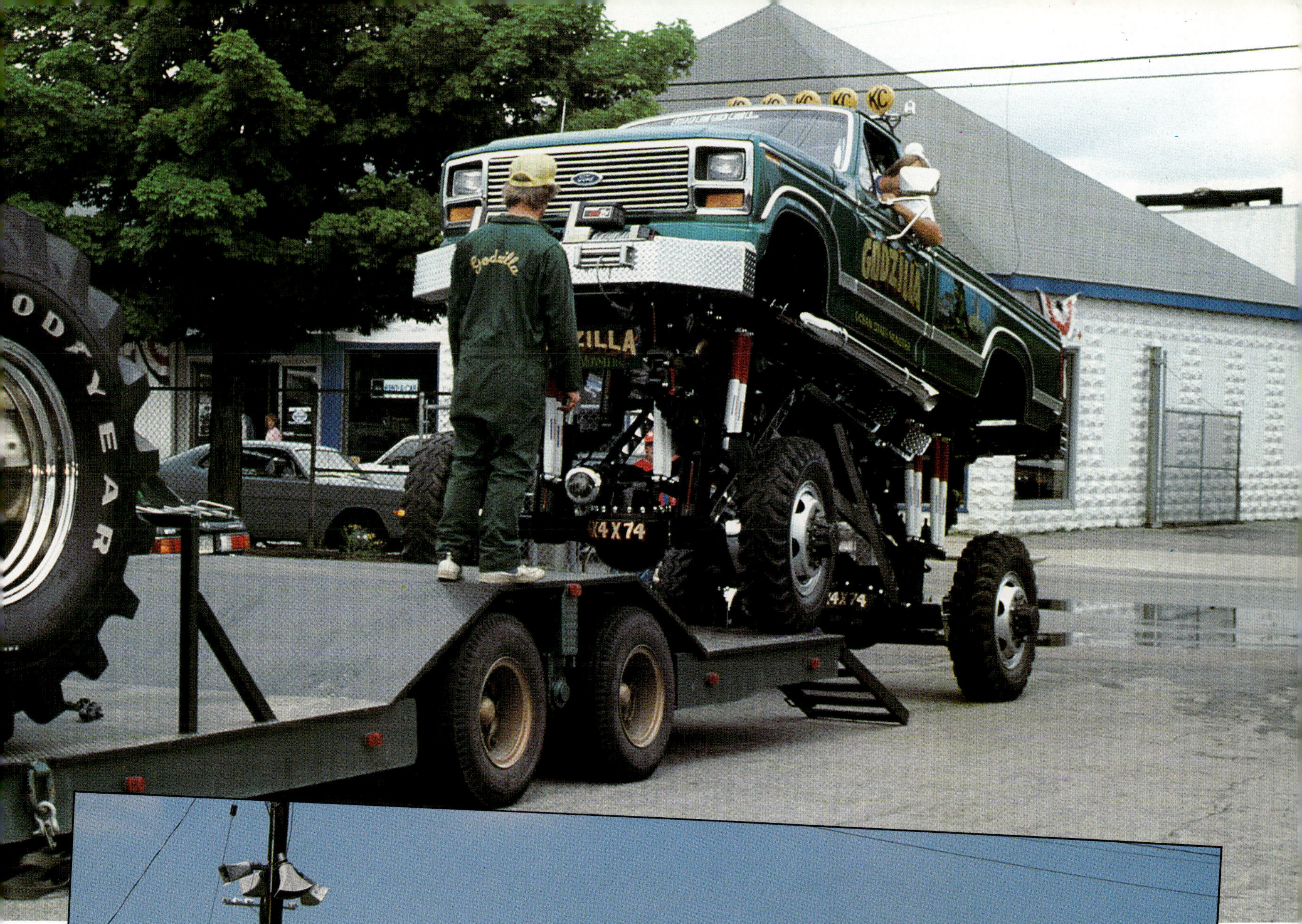
Godzilla
GODZILLA

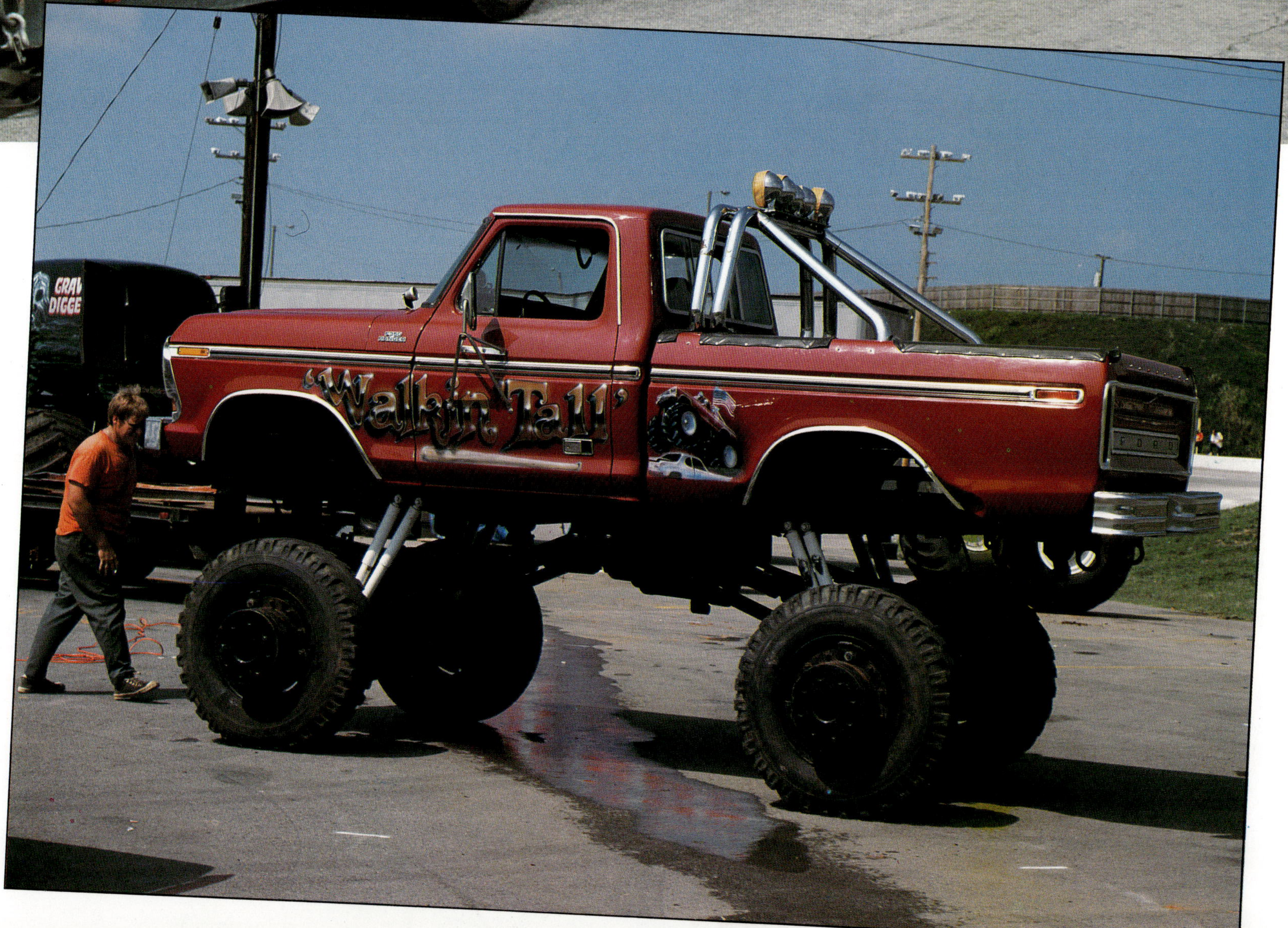
'Walkin' Tall'

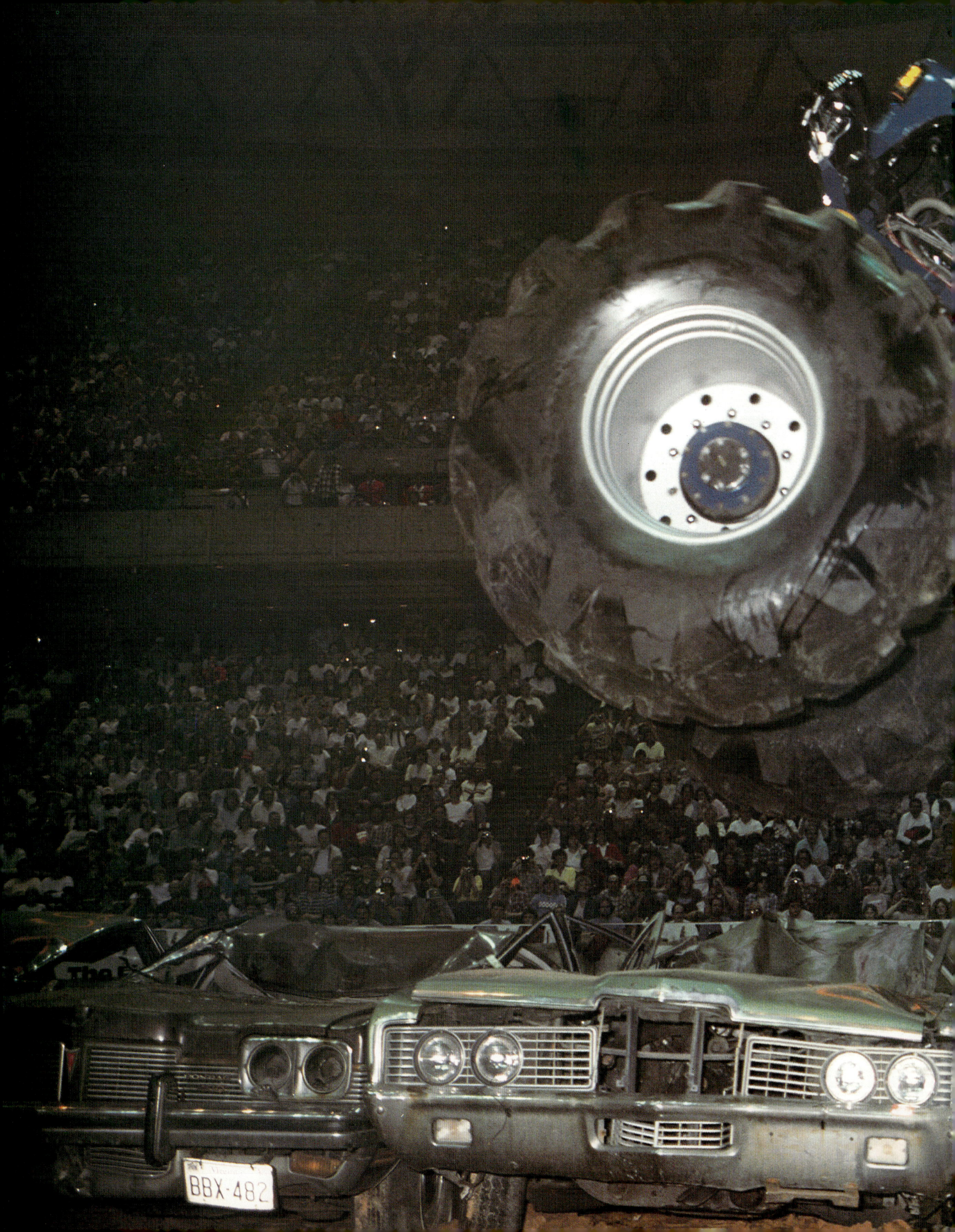
BBX-482

It's Showtime

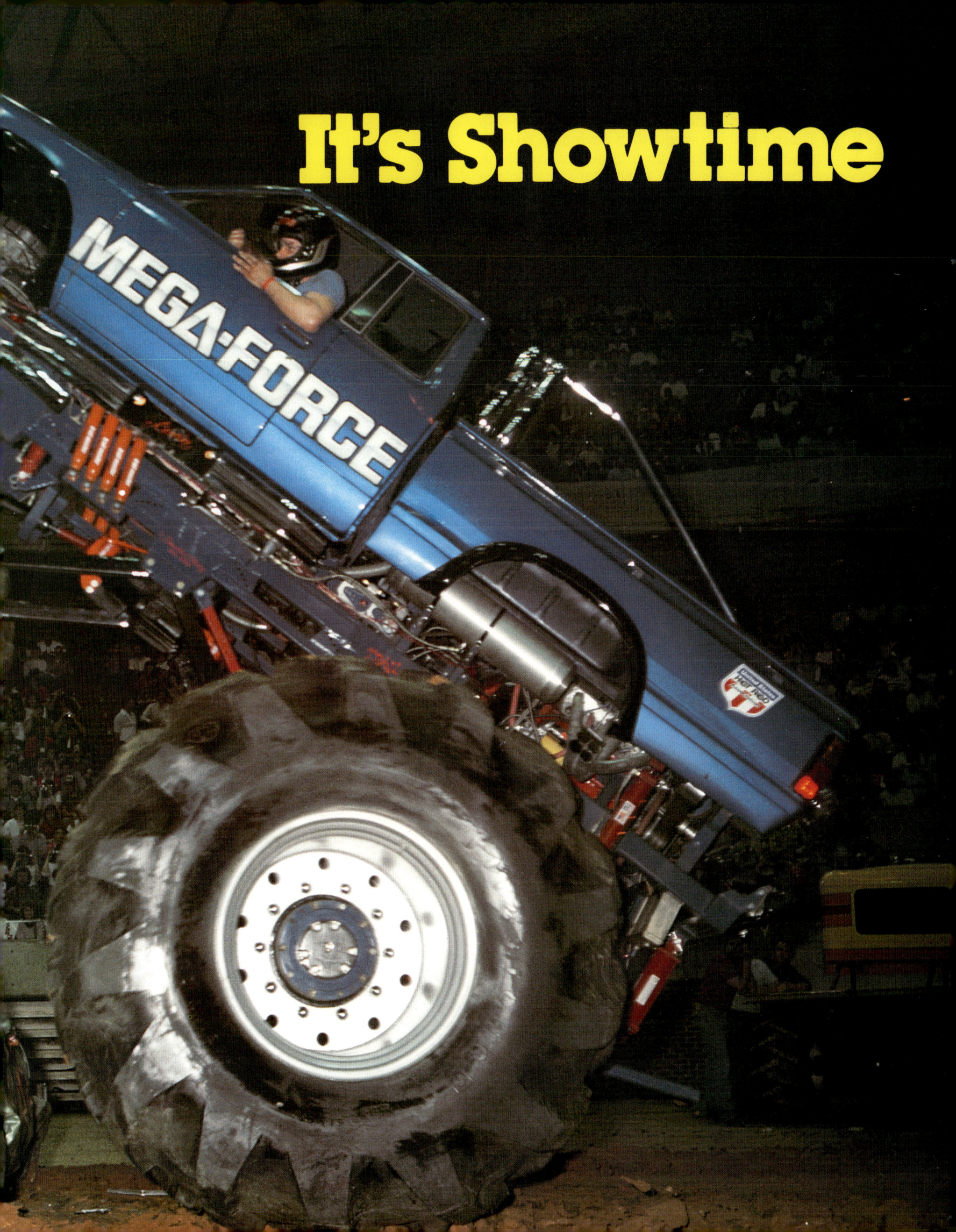

38 Monster Trucks

What good is a monster truck if one can't play with it? There's nothing worse than having an 80,000 dollar white elephant taking up a large portion of the driveway. For the longest time, a monster truck's claim to fame was its size and the rather mundane fact that it was steerable from both the front and the back. But people become bored easily, and to just roll around on 48-, 66- or 73-inch tires wasn't enough to keep the hearts pounding forever.

Since this is a world where 'he who has the best gimmick wins,' it wasn't long before the nimble minds of monster truck owners shifted into high gear to come up with innovative uses for the monsters. There is some debate as to who was first to park his monster truck on top of a bunch of abandoned clunkers, but *Bigfoot's* name seems to come to the surface more often than not. According to Bill Candela, Vice President of Bigfoot, Inc, 'There might have been some other truck who did the car crushing first in their backyard, but we did the first one in front of a paying crowd in Jefferson City, Missouri, back in 1982.'

Don't think everything always goes as planned in the world of *Bigfoot* either. That first night, the old cars were placed ever so slightly apart, causing the big blue Ford truck to slip between them, breaking a driveline part.

Pages 36-37: A closer look at *Mega-Force* will show that there are two engines powering the mini-bodied monster. Both are Chevies.

Above: The only monster capable of doing a 300-foot wheelie – *Aces High*.

Below: All a blur was Bob Chandler's *Bigfoot* in action at a monster truck hill climb.

Right: Dust flies as the *Ice Monster* speeds along the track.

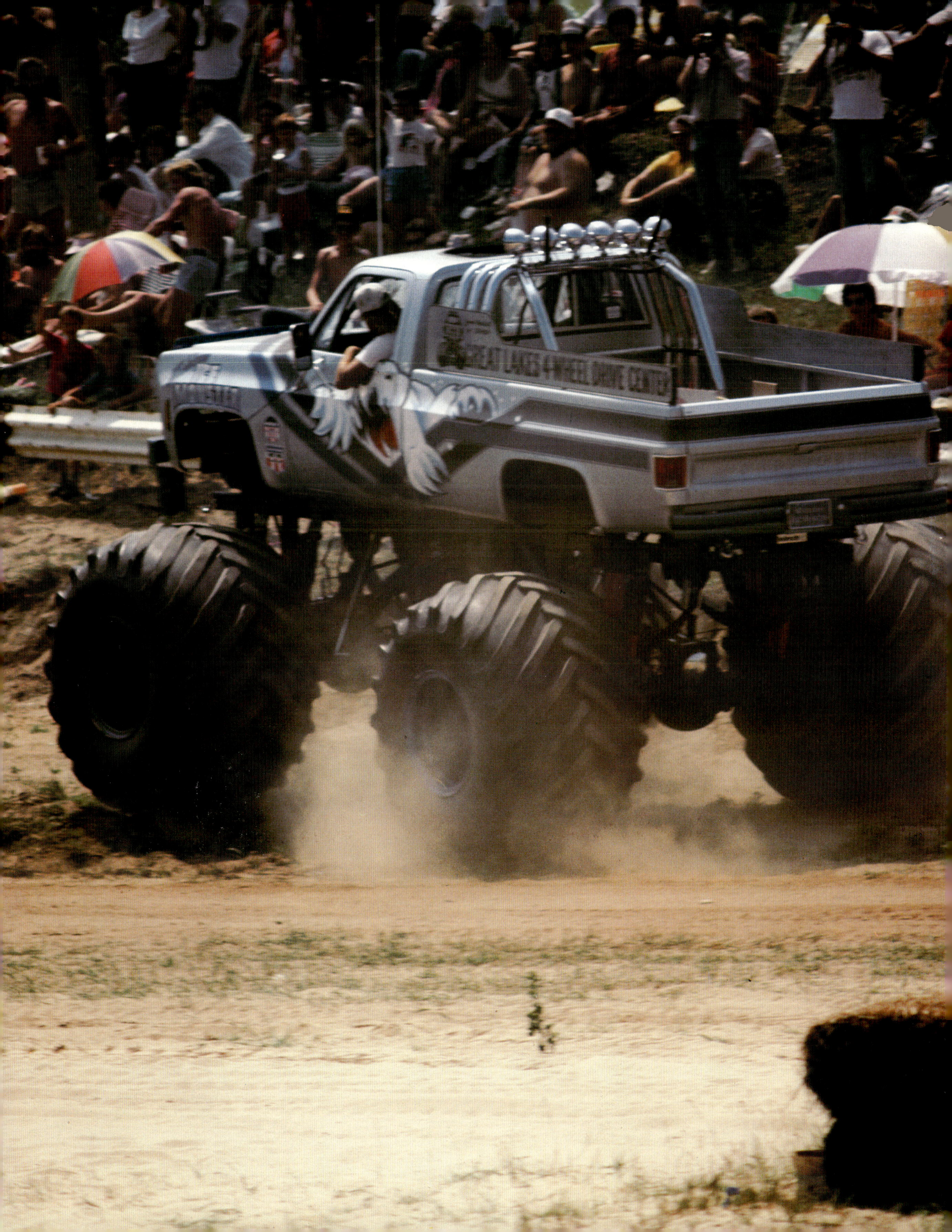
GREAT LAKES 4-WHEEL DRIVE CENTER

Bigfoot was hustled back to the Hazelwood shop where repairs were made. The next day, Chandler returned to Jefferson City to do another show. Car crushing was born!

As is the case with most anything, everyone else jumped on the bandwagon once word of *Bigfoot's* success got out. Monster trucks everywhere followed *Bigfoot's* lead and flying glass filled the air from coast to coast. But what appears to be a simple feat of making flat cars out of round cars is really a lot more scientific than meets the eye

Getting the right cars to crush can make the show a promoters' dream. Larry Tura *(Hercules)* likes two-door hard tops, preferably GM cars because their roof designs make for easy collapsing. Then there's Willie Townes whose *Virginia Beach Beast* sports tank tread. He doesn't care what type of cars they bring. Station wagons offer a different problem because of their extra length; they can be used only with other wagons and not with any other kind of car. Keeping the cars the same length, type and pre-crush condition is paramount to the monster truck driver—and it shoud be to the promoter—to ensure a good performance for his bill-paying patrons.

Of note here is what the crews do to the cars before the giant Goodyears make metal pancakes out of them. First, all four tires are chocked (usually the monster truck crews carry their own chocks) on all four corners. Next in line for an early demise is the radio antenna and the air cleaner stud. These two items could offer a monster truck driver a punctured tire if not removed prior to his assault.

There are variations of the car-crushing scene too. Jack Willman from Madison, Illinois, was the first to crush old buses, with his famed *Taurus* Chevy. Preparation for this feat is similar to that for the cars, except that Jack does some interior work on the bus that he won't divulge. A couple of other monster trucks have tried the bus routine with near disastrous results, leaving Jack and *Taurus* to still be the only currently successful truck doing buses.

'There's more than one way to tear up a car,' says monster truck owner Alan Tura *(Goliath)* of Warren, Ohio. A further extension of car crushing has been the tearing apart of a car. Alan explains, 'You take a scrap car with some decay, chain one end of it to a pulling sled and the other chain I hook to my truck. Give it about three feet

Taking along a passenger was once a regular occurence, but insurance and safety regulations have made it a rarity.

Inset: Hill climbs are one of few stunts that monsters don't master with ease. Even *Bigfoot* has trouble.

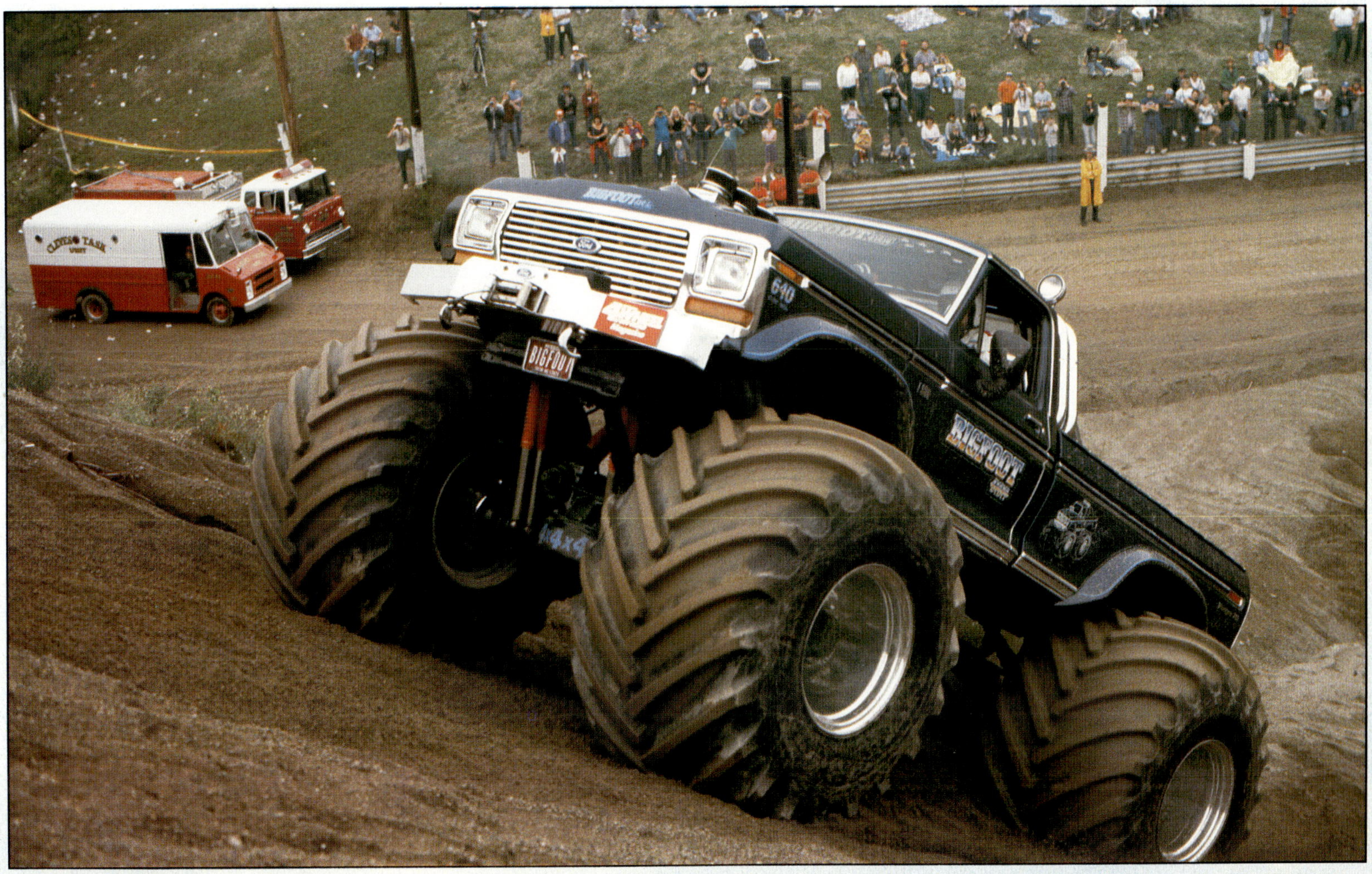
BIGFOOT

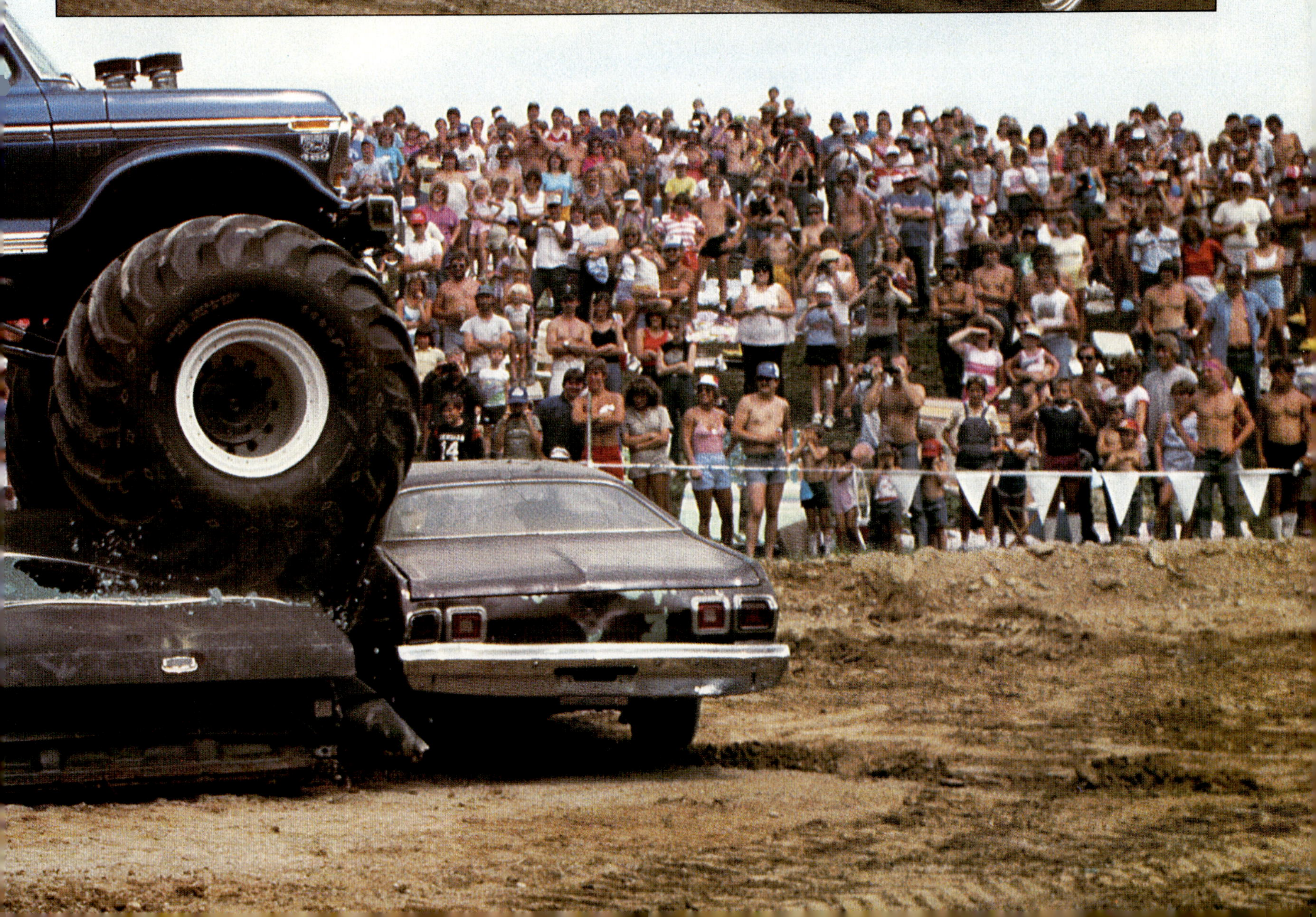

of slack in the chain and when my 15,000 pound truck takes off, something has to give. More than likely the car gets torn in two pieces. We do this, I'll admit, with unibody cars. Full-frame cars sometimes present problems.' This trick has also become popular with promoters who can get Fred Shafer (*Bearfoot*) and Jack Willman (*Taurus*) together. The two men were once partners on the original *Bearfoot*. Getting the pair together to compete, or pull cars apart, has produced some of the more exciting action in all of monster truckdom.

Through all of this car crushing, though, comes one burning question: Why is it the single most requested exploit of the monster trucks? What makes the masses come unglued when the monsters crash down on worn out old junkers that once would have rusted quietly away? Car crushing is so popular that in the movie *Cannonball Run II*, *Bigfoot* was paid a substantial amount of money to drive over the top of a new Porsche! What is it that makes car crushing numero uno with fans both young and old?

Bob George, President of SRO Promotions, the leading promoter of truck pull events and the user of more monster trucks than any other promoter in the world, explains it this way. 'I think it comes from a fantasy of everyone who has ever been caught in rush hour traffic in a big city, or been stuck behind a slow driver on a country road. The desire is to be able to drive over top of them and be on your merry way. The monster trucks fulfill that fantasy with a bang. And as for the kids and teenagers that attend our over 200 events a year, we think it's the raw power they produce that brings the teen crowd and the youngsters .... Well, kids like anything that's loud, fast and destructive.'

Monster truck driver Diehl Wilson (*Virginia Giant*) concurred, then added, 'I think too, that more people are buying pickup trucks than ever before, and they see the monster trucks as an extension of their truck. Brand identification is also a very important part of our industry.' Be it with a Ford, Chevy, Dodge, Jeep or any of the various monster vehicles that are around, the fact is that crushing cars is number one with the fans and as long as there are abandoned cars around, these guys are in business.

A rather freak accident recently happened that changed the complexion of monster truck car crushing. It was kind of accident that people dream of, like playing the wrong number in the lottery and having it hit for four million dollars—that kind of accident! Jack Willman and Fred Shafer (*Bearfoot*) had just completed their newest creation, *Lil Bearfoot*, a Chevy S-20, and hit the throttle of the supercharged big-block Chevy mill. Instead of climbing the cars instantly, the S-10 reared back on its giant back tires like a dog begging for food. Sensing the impending disaster, Willman let off the throttle and the blue Chevy came crashing down on top of the cars. After idling off the cars, Jack and Fred sat mystified as they watched the videotape of the 'Flight of *Lil Bearfoot*,' wondering what went wrong. Speculating that it was the

Top left: The *Michigan Ice Monster* draws attention just driving along the side of the track.

Left: The Chevy of Everett Jasmer dwarfs people standing nearby. This overhead view really shows the size of the monster trucks.

Above: Many car dealers have used the monsters to attract customers into their lots.

Right: Hooked to a sled, *Bigfoot* shows just what it can do. Pulling fans enjoy seeing the monsters do something other than just crushing cars.

44   Monster Trucks

Above: The massive 10-foot-tall tires that only *Bigfoot* has came from Alaska where they were used on the vehicles that delivered the pipeline equipment across the tundra.

Right: The *Grave Digger* of Dennis Anderson started off as a mud race truck but was quickly converted to car mashing. The engine is mounted in the rear.

Far right: Gary Bauer perfected the reverse wheelstand with his *Lon-Ranger* Ford. Now almost all the monsters do them.

It's Showtime

Wheelies were an important part of the drag racing scene back in the mid-sixties. The drag racing Funny Car had been born and the Big Three car manufacturers were vying for sales by supporting drag racing teams around the country. For various drivers they had built a special one-of-a-kind series of cars that had a 'funny' look to them. The majority had altered wheelbases that took on a rather bizarre appearance. During this period the factories were rolling out experimental cars in hopes of getting a leg up on the accelerating competition. One of the cars produced by Chrysler Corporation was tested and found to be too light in the front end, causing it to lift skyward under hard acceleration. Chrysler engineers initially were perplexed over the car's airborne exploits. However, PR Department brass realized that they might have the coup of the year. Why not build the car to do quarter-mile wheelstands? They did, and the results have changed the course of drag racing history. It carried over some 22 years later into monster trucks.

Butler, Pennslyvania's Jake Henke wanted a monster truck, but he didn't want one like everyone else's. Jake took his show-winning Chevy El Camino and did a major face-lift to make it not just a monster truck but a bumper-dragging, tire-smoking show-worthy monster truck. His *Aces High* El Camino is all that and more. The truck can carry the massive front tires six feet in the air for 300 + feet even in the snow or rain. Combined with the glistening chrome and deep candy blue and gold paint, this is one unique wheelstanding monster truck.

That first wheelstand the *Lil Bearfoot* did should have been an omen of another aspect of the wheelstand things to happen. As more and more monster trucks got into the wheelstand market, the natural competitive rivalry came into play. Outdoing the other trucks became an obsession with many of the owners, especially in the case of *Bigfoot*. To outshine *Bigfoot* became the prime motivation of many a monster truck driver, so much so that wreckless abandon took over. The logical conclusion was that it was just a matter of time before disaster struck. And it did in Philadelphia, where a standing-room-only crowd gasped in disbelief when *Quadzilla*, a monster truck based on a Jeep, rolled over backwards when momentum from his wheelstand sent him sprawling. No serious injuries were sustained in the crash. Just two months later, *Bearfoot* suffered the same fate while performing in Colorado. Luckily there too, only ego and the Chevy truck were damaged.

SRO/USHRA Off-Road Shows Technical Director George Carpenter must have had the powers of ESP. Just four months before, Carpenter and other officials at SRO/USHRA, had set up safety rules and mechanical guidelines for the monster trucks. Carpenter commented on the matter: 'We just knew that with the competition between the monster trucks getting so intense, it was only a matter of time before something bad would happen unless we set up safety rules and regulations for the monster trucks.' Those rules have kept a lid on things, but they haven't kept the monster trucks' wheels on the ground.

Head-to-head competition between the trucks became the next logical step. Figuring a way to do it was something in itself, and SRO President Bob George is credited by many as the brains behind the monster truck obstacle course competition. The idea and the execution were quite simple. First the course had to be laid out, determined primarily by how much room was available.

It's Showtime

Left: After crossing the man-made hill, *Hercules* hits the cars for his turn at the obstacle course.

Above: Side-by-side hill-climbing and drag-racing are just two of the many things that the promoters ask and demand of the monster truck drivers.

When space was no problem, as in the major stadiums that many of the promoters were using, a starting line was selected. That was usually at the same place that the pull would call its starting line. About 60 feet down the track two to four old cars would be placed as the first jump. Once cleared, a straight stretch would give the trucks a chance to showcase their acceleration before they would have to go over a rather steep hill, often becoming airborne in the process. Back down to earth, they would straighten out, go another stretch and then cross a few more cars before coming to rest at the top of one more hill. Variations would be thrown in such as going through a mud bog or having to pull the sled 100 feet.

Sometimes the winner will be determined by the elapsed time that it takes for the truck to complete the course, but more often than not the promoter would have the crowd's applause be the deciding factor as to who the winner would be.

Getting the crowd involved is also a stroke of promotional genius. TNT, Inc's Tom Carter says, 'Anytime you can get the fans involved with the event, the better off you are. They feel like they're important and they have some bearing on the outcome. We've also found they stay for the entire pull if they know they're needed. It also takes a little pressure off us to decide a winner.'

The obstacle courses have also brought up the quality of the monster trucks because the drivers know that to win means more bookings from the promotors. To win these events also means their trucks have to be in A-1 condition and running at the top of their game. You can't fool the public—especially up to 75,000 of them all at once.

Since the monster trucks many times appear with truck and tractor pulls, it's not surprising that the high-risers would also be asked to hook up to the pulling sleds. *Bearfoot* owner and driver Fred Shafer says that the sled-pulling is one of the hardest things that the trucks are asked to do. Shafer explained, 'It's hard enough on the motors to just get those big wheels turning. Pulling the sled, though, really puts great pressure on the vehicle. Any time you have to put the pedal to the metal, the motor really takes a lot of punishment.'

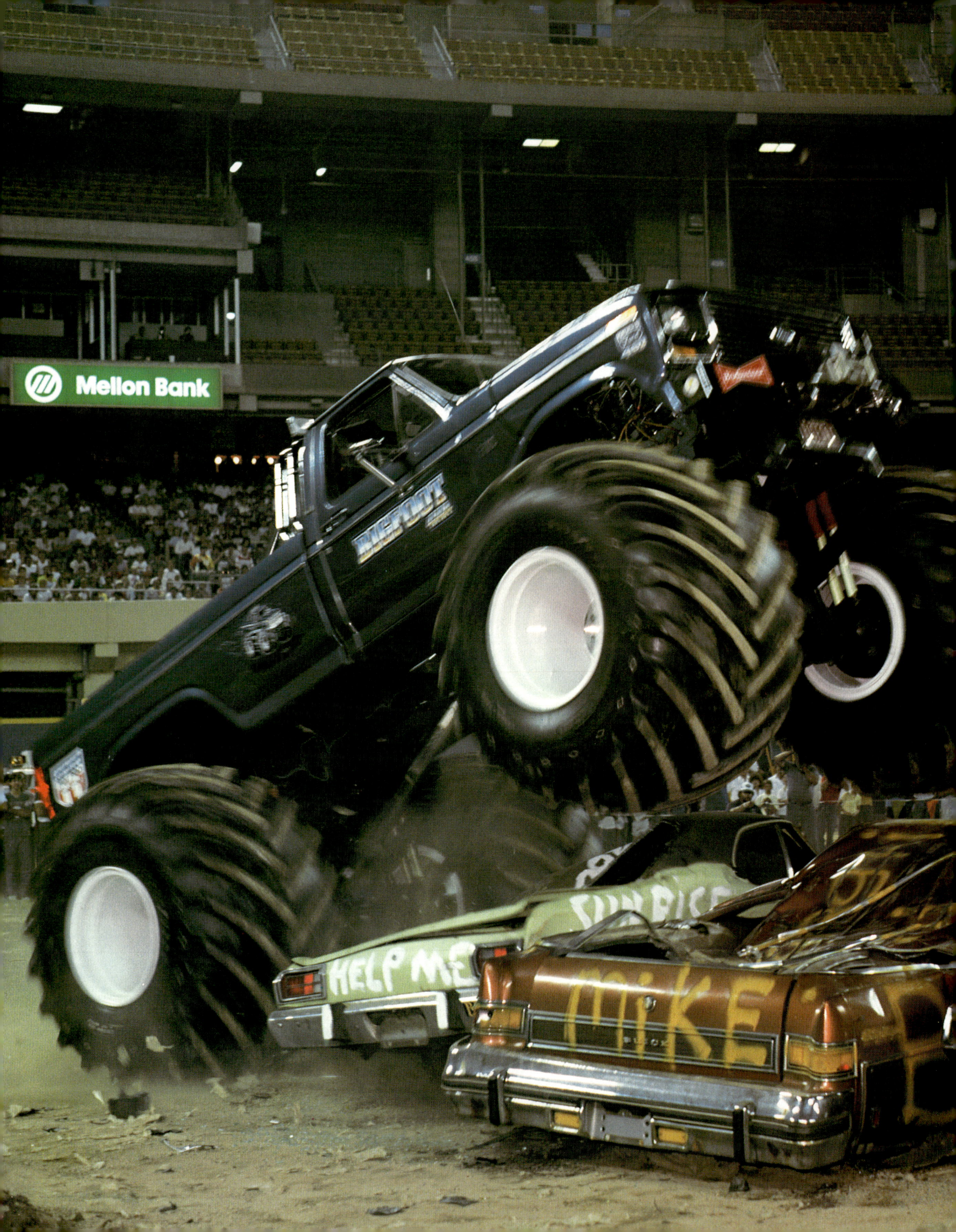
Mellon Bank
BIGFOOT
HELP ME
MIKE

It's Showtime 49

As usual, *Bigfoot* was the first to hook to a pulling sled and make a run. Knowing that this was going to happen sooner or later, the people at *Bigfoot* outfitted one of their six *Bigfoot* trucks with a planetary rear end assembly, one that allowed the truck to do wheelstands as it went down track. A little help from the man riding the sled was required to help the giant truck get the wheels up by just riding the brakes of the weight transfer machine. The first time this was accomplished, as usual, the fans in attendance went berserk. Predictably, many monster trucks have gone to the planetary rear ends since then.

One of the wildest tricks the trucks have been performing recently is jumping from ramps to the ground. Larry Tura of the *Hercules* truck explained that some of his jumps have been as high as eight feet off the ground. One can certainly understand that the trucks' suspension systems are tested to the limit on such maneuvers. Tura explained that his truck body had been beaten up, and that he had seen other trucks actually twist their frames on some of the tricks. Up until recently, most monster truck drivers would have told you that the tires are the most reliable component on their trucks. Not any longer. The big jumps the trucks are making these days have actually burst the big tires, and crushed or bent the wheels supporting them. Something's got to give sometimes when that kind of weight hits the ground. What else the monsters are going to be asked to perform remains to be seen. It's certainly gotten to the point where 'the wilder the better' is the keynote with these gangly machines. More and more, the monster trucks are being brought together in large numbers to challenge each other.

Left: Only a trained eye could tell one *Bigfoot* from the others. That's part of the plan, so that everyone who sees the trucks will remember them.

Above: Lights on top of a monster are for more than just show and a sponsor. Night events can be tricky and the extra lights can make the difference.

One of the most interesting of those multi-truck events took place at the famous 180-foot-high hill in Cleves, Ohio, during the summer of 1986. For many years, the four-wheel-drive trucks have been trying—with very few successes—to make it to the top of the giant hill in Cleves. The big problem with the hill of course, is that it's made completely from pea gravel. It's like climbing a hill made of marbles. Chandler had long been fascinated with the hill and wondered what his truck would do on the incline. The challenge event of the big hill featured some ten monsters ready to try it. *Bigfoot* was the only one of the group that was able to make it to the top, but it wasn't that easy, even for the great original. On this occasion the trucks also participated in another riveting contest—drag-racing! Only in this particular case, it was done uphill on one of the smaller hills at the Cleves course. Is there anything that won't be tried by the imaginative owners of the trucks?

Looking at these monsters, one has to believe that they could really make great mud vehicles. With those tires, they should really be something. The prospect of cleaning them up would be enough to stop many of the trucks, but still, there have been a number of them that have run in the mud. The *Stomper Bully* of the TNT sanctioning body is one of the best in the business of getting through the slop. Another observation about the trucks is that they look buoyant enough to float. And float they do, as has been proved on a number of occasions. There have been races across rivers and lakes, with the monsters' cleated wheels acting as sort of paddlewheels for locomotion.

But there had also been one unfortunate monster water truck that didn't quite do what was planned. The *Cardiff Giant* monster truck received a ton of national media attention when it slowly turned completely over in 1985 in Rena, Nevada. It was an amazing sight, as all that remained of the truck in view was a small portion of each of all four wheels protruding from the water. Yes, they do float!

Monster truck owners become fanatics on the capabilities of their machines. There even have been challenges issued by one truck owner to another, some of which have been accepted. It all makes for great fun, and also puts thousands of fans in the stands.

Fred Shafer says, though, that not all of the ever-growing number of monster trucks is going to survive. The reason, he believes, is that many of the builders just don't have the expertise to build their trucks to withstand the tremendous punishment. 'Only the strong will survive what is being asked of them these days,' he comments. 'It's all-out competition the fans want to see from us these days. I really don't know where it's all going to end.'

Above left: Some monsters aren't 'true' monsters; many are just a big set of tires and nothing more.

Top: There aren't many names left from the monster movies. Cliff Starbird owns *Frankenstein*.

Right: One of the first car monsters was the Camaro of K Dabney from North Carolina. Dabney's car immediately became one of the most sought-after monsters.

Monsters in the Public Eye

Anytime something catches on, you can bet your last dollar that there will be enterprising souls there in line to imitate. Monster trucks have seen just that happen to them on a grand scale.

Many experts in the industry credit *Bigfoot's* role in the movie *Take This Job and Shove It* as the jumping-off point for the monster trucks, in that it gave a true visual picture of the truck's performance capabilities. More important, though, was the actual amount of time *Bigfoot* was on camera. This was not a cameo role. After this film the doors swung open and a flood of products, videos and toys emerged.

The toy industry was quick to see that kids of all ages were fascinated by the big trucks. Contracts with Playskool, Schaper, Lewis Galoob, Nylint and many more put *Bigfoot, Stomper Bully, Bearfoot,* Spiker's *All-American* and *Eagle, USA-1* and *Ertl's Intimidator* onto shelves everywhere. Not only are they in assemble-it-yourself kit form, they also come motorized, battery operated, friction-propelled and radio-controlled. The famed Matchbox Company, long the leader in miniature toys, countered with their own series of eight monster trucks in 1:64 scale. So big was the toy market that *Bigfoot's* founder, Bob Chandler, put together his own line of merchandise and hired people to sell both the merchandise and licensing rights to his name for anything and everything.

For the past two years the video scene and monster trucks have been running neck and neck in the race to see which one is the hottest commodity, so it's only logical that the two forces should team up from time to time. The most notable comes from the MTV-VH-1 world where the ZZ Top rock group featured *Bearfoot* almost the entire two and a half minutes in a rock video. The Granite City, Illinois-based Chevy was put through its paces, doing everything a good monster truck is built to do. Not to be outdone, *Bigfoot* starred, with a group called UTFO, in a music video.

Monster trucks have starred in their own video specials as well. Most notable is the three-part series produced by Mediacast TV from Chicago that teamed with SRO/USHRA Promotions and the syndicated TV series, *The Superchargers*, to tape the 'Battle of the Monster Trucks,' 'Revenge of the Monster Trucks' and the 'Final Chapter.' The first show started off as just a half-hour segment of *The Supercharger,* but ratings in the major markets where the series aired yielded big numbers and so producers added more footage and released the BETA/VHS versions to the public. Sales were brisk.

Not to be outdone, both SRO/USHRA and United Sports of America (USA) promptly produced their own videos showcasing their events with heavy emphasis on the monster trucks in action. The tapes, about 30 to 40 minutes long, have rock sound tracks with spectacular footage. TNT Inc, the third largest promoter of pulling, mud and monster truck events, is currently working on a tape for release. It appears that the popularity of both the monster trucks and the video shorts has made for a double-barrelled commercial success for the two diverse industries.

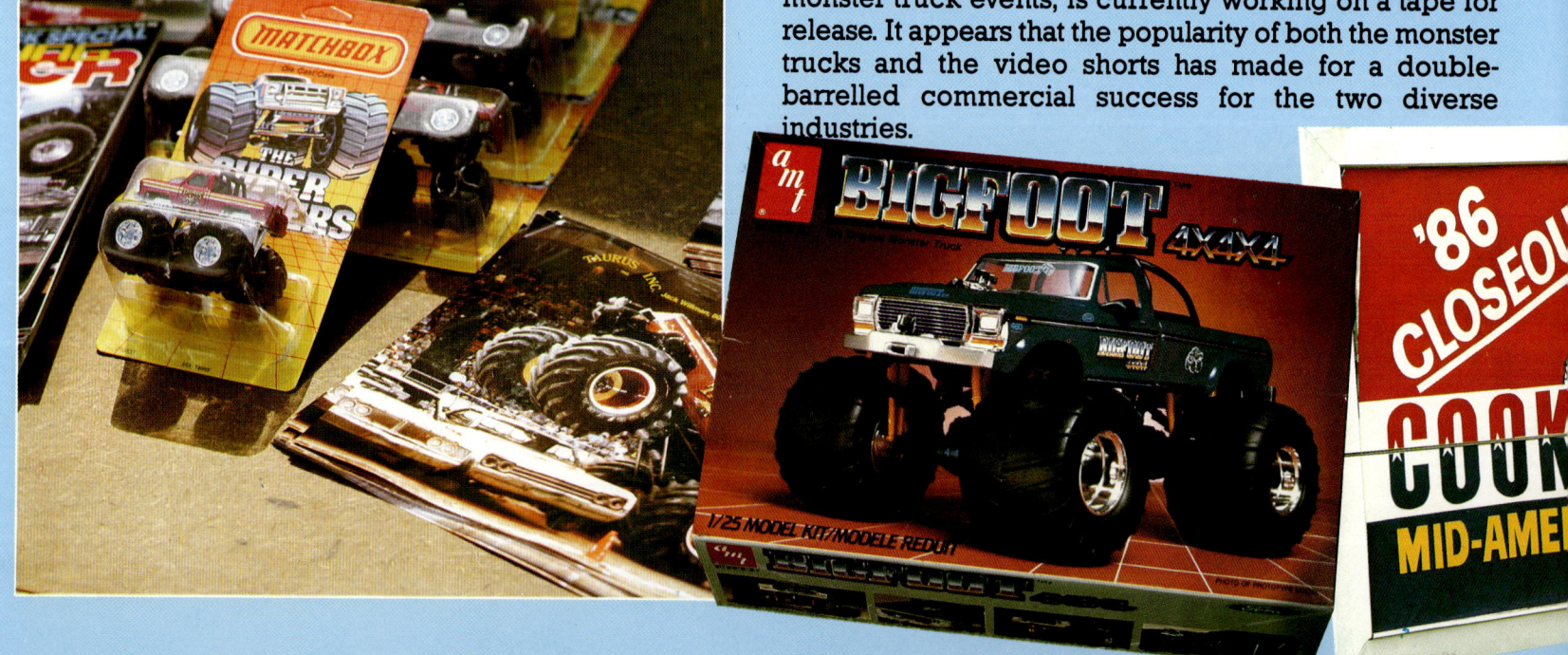

Monsters in the Public Eye

The word 'commercial' has another role here, too. The television moguls were a little slower than normal to get in gear as far as taking advantage of the monster trucks' popularity. It's not for certain who was first to use a monster truck in a television commercial, but *Bigfoot* has appeared in two so far. One was for *Bigfoot* sponsor Ford Motor Company and the other was for Duracell batteries showing a Playskool *Bigfoot* scooting across the floor. True Value Hardware stores end their TV commercial with their sponsored monster truck *USA-1* crashing down on top of some old cars. This commercial was well thought out as the last frame of the 30-second spot freezes the *USA-1* Chevy in mid-air and leaves one wanting more.

Nondescript are the monster trucks used in filming a fast-paced Mountain Dew soft drink commercial. The editing is so quick that trying to identify the monster trucks used is virtually impossible. Still the effect and the message is clear: monster truck drivers and off-road fans drink Mountain Dew. Fram Oil Filters also uses an unidentified monster truck in its national ad. The message seems to be that this product can handle the tough lubrication jobs, and the monster truck certainly demonstrates that point.

Monster trucks have permeated every form of the media with the possible exception of radio. Of course, event advertisements, broadcasting where the monsters are scheduled to perform, is conveyed even over the radio. But a monster truck is a visual thing and must be seen and heard to be appreciated. About the only place one can escape their presence today might be on the moon!

Far left: Monster trucks are everywhere at a recent tractor pull concession shack. The current rage appears on the covers of magazines, as toys and as posters.

Center left: The *Bigfoot* comes in kit form and is on the shelves all over the nation.

Left: The Cook Truck Ranch in Evansville, Indiana, uses a monster truck drawing in its road sign advertisement.

Above: The mini *Bearfoot* is almost an exact scale replica of the real thing. The smaller version is extremely popular with the kids.

Odd Balls

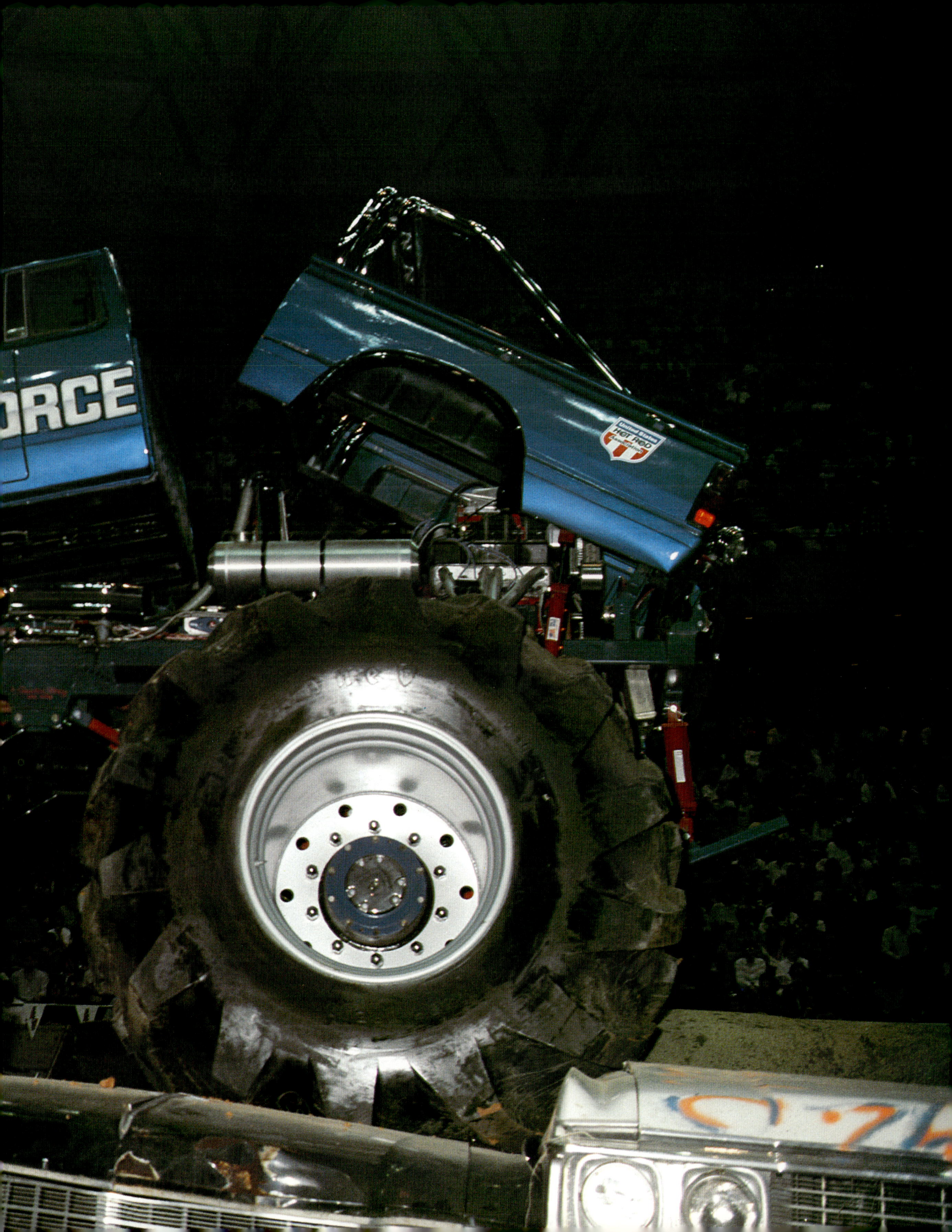
ORCE

MUSTANG
1967
PONY EXPRESS
Built & Operated by Tommy Bryant
Pensacola, Fla.

Odd Balls 57

Pages 54-55: The *Mega-Force* is one of the first – but certainly not the last – awesome two-engine monster trucks. It's certainly not short on power.

The *Pony Express* is a Mustang body mounted on big wheels.

Right: The *Virginia Beach Beast* is a strange monster. The vehicle is mounted on top of a tank chassis and also carries actual tank treads.

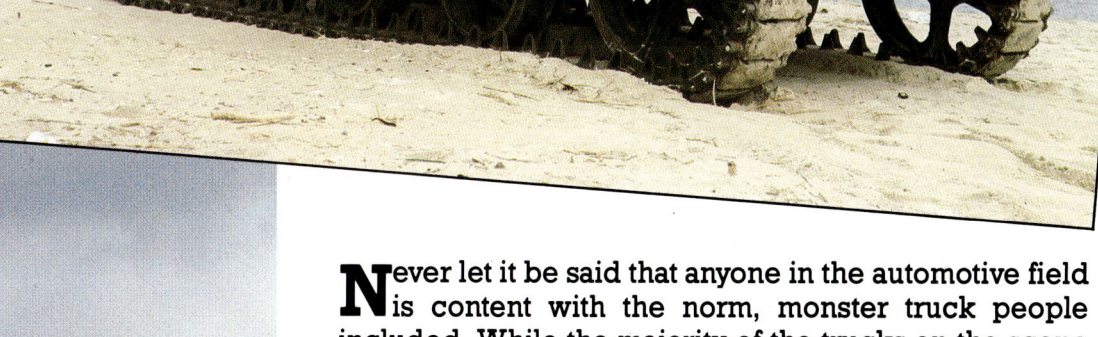

Never let it be said that anyone in the automotive field is content with the norm, monster truck people included. While the majority of the trucks on the scene are the more traditional pickup truck variety, there are a few which are a touch more, like, radical?

The first that comes to mind is the *Virginia Beach Beast* of Willie Townes of Norfolk, Virginia. Willie's Chevy Blazer body is mounted on top of a tank chassis complete with rubberized tank treads. This truck will go over the top of anything you put in front of it and has become one of the most popular monster trucks in the industry. Unique also is the way Townes has elected to steer the massive machine. He tried a conventional steering wheel with Chevy power steering units, but he wasn't happy with that system. So he went to the stock tank controls with levers similar to those of a bulldozer.

The big semi trucks are a hot item with motorsports enthusiasts, so it was only logical that someone would build a monster semi, and Don Puchholtz of Wyoming, Iowa has done just that. His *King of the Road* Peterbuilt semi operates off of an FMC 6-wheel frame and stands about 13 feet high. Although it won't do the conventional wheelstand like most monster trucks, the *King* does hook to the pulling sled and can carry the front end.

There are also a number of vans on the scene that draw a lot of attention because of their uniqueness. From the East there's the *Heavy Metal* Ford of Mike Trinagel from, of all places, the Bronx, New York. All the way across country is a trio of monster vans: Tom Feeny's *Led Butterfly*, which calls Portland, Oregon home, the 1976 Ford *Quadravan*, one of the most colorful of all the trucks,

KC
Maaco
RUGGED TRAIL
SUSPENSIONS
ATI
AUTOMATIC TRANSMISSION
Kendall GT-1

Odd Balls 59

Left: Another two-engine monster truck, *Goliath* shows off its big wheels.

Right: Bob Chandler has done it again by installing an additional four of the giant ten-foot tires on one of his many big-wheel trucks.

with its wild multi-hued paint job, and the *Barbarian* Van of Bruce Gault of San Jose, California. Bruce recently took on an extensive tour of South America. Also from the shores of California is the van of Jim Oldaker. Jim's *Rollin' Thunder* is different not only in that it's a van but that he uses a Detroit Diesel for power.

Between the monster van and semi is the rather strange 6-wheel monster truck of Charles Flynn of Henagar, Alabama. Mounted atop a custom-built frame is a late-model Chevy Crew Cab body that even has a sleeper attached where back seat passengers would normally sit.

If one is good then two must be better, according to monster truck driver/builder Kevin Dabney of Fayetteville, North Carolina. Kevin's *Blue Thunder* Camaro is one of a few car monsters out there, but his real claim to fame is his twin engine *Mega-Force* Nissan truck. Mounted in the bed of the Nissan mini truck is a blown big block Chevy, another one rests in the stock location under the hood. Alan Tura also sports two engines in his new *Goliath*. Using car bodies on monsters has been gaining in popularity. The most renowned of all the car monsters is Cliff Starbird's gorgeous candy apple red monster 'Vette. The Kansas native was one of the first to put a car body on a monster truck frame and his success was instantaneous. Not so well known as Cliff Starbird, but headed in that direction, is Mart Williams, whose *Cajun King* 1976 Cadillac has started to appear everywhere and make quite a name for itself.

No one machine stands out for its workmanship more than Randy Weber's *Brutte Boss Hogg*. Weber, who lives in Bristol, Indiana, hand-built his 'truckor,' as he calls it, in his own garage. The body has no resemblance to any production line truck made and that's the way Weber wanted it. It defies description other than it is a classic piece of work inside and out.

Be it a twin engine truck or a semi, Corvette or Caddy, *King Kong* or *King Krunch*, you can bet on one thing for sure. The monster trucks will continue to come in all shapes and sizes.

Monster Trucks Illustrated

USA-1

Monster Trucks

KING KRUNCH

SAMSON

Monster Trucks Illustrated 63

GODZILLA

THUMPER

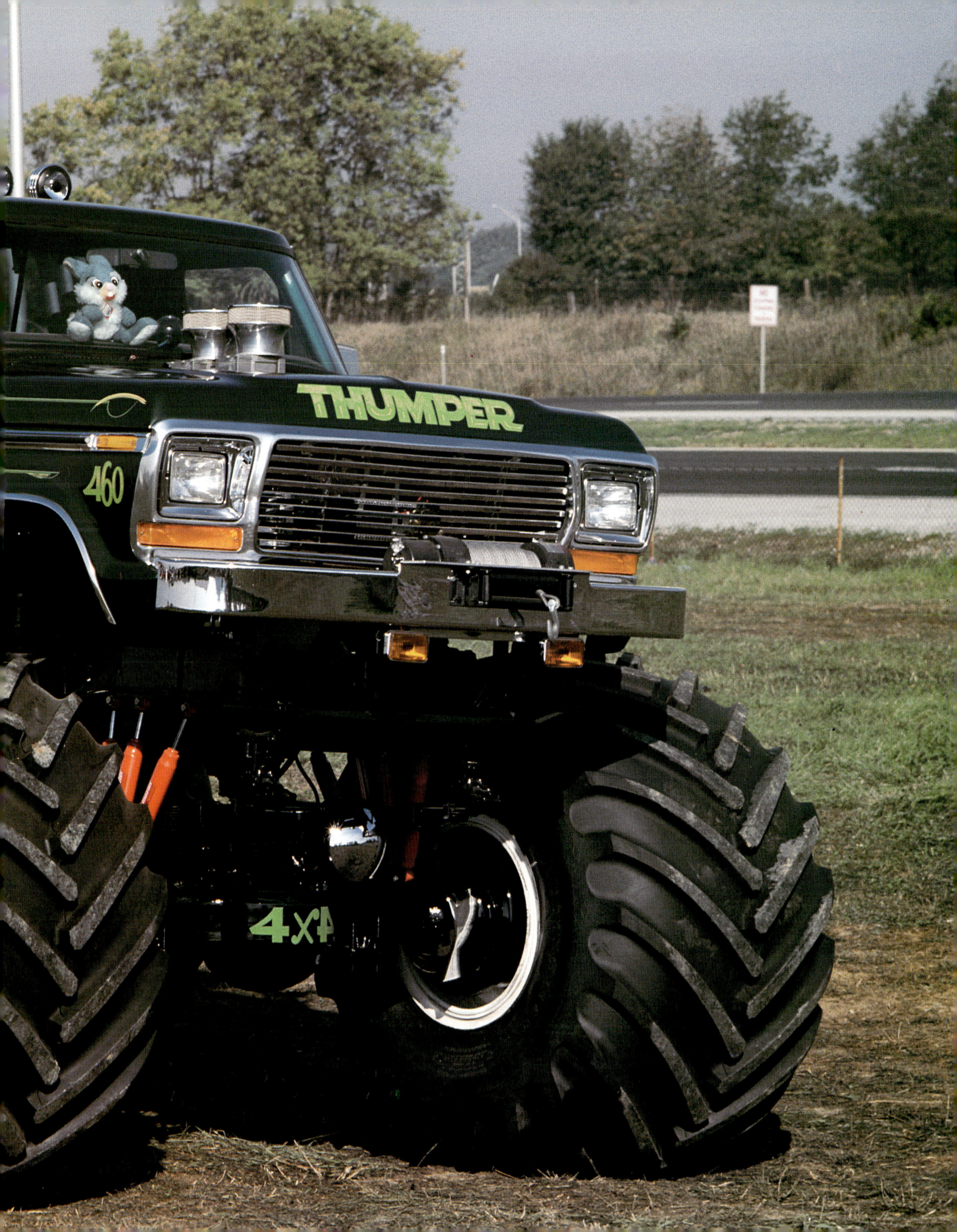
THUMPER
460

66 Monster Trucks

MONSTER VETTE

OUTLAW 35

HERCULES

BEAST

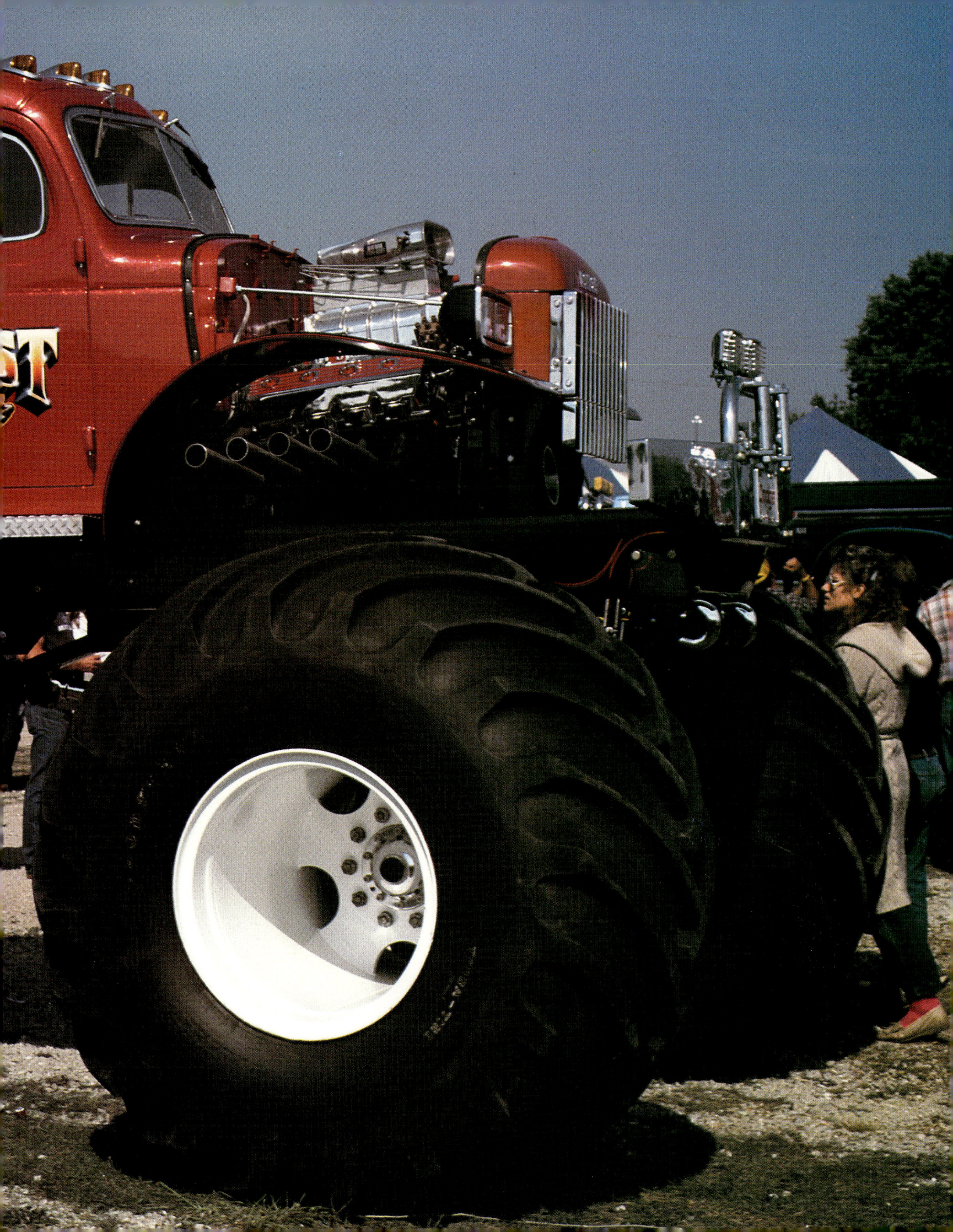

GENTLE BEN

HERCULES (MAROON)

Monster Trucks — 70

Monster Trucks Illustrated 71

SOUTHERN NIGHTMARE

BIGFOOT

ICE MONSTER

SKOAL BANDIT

GOLIATH

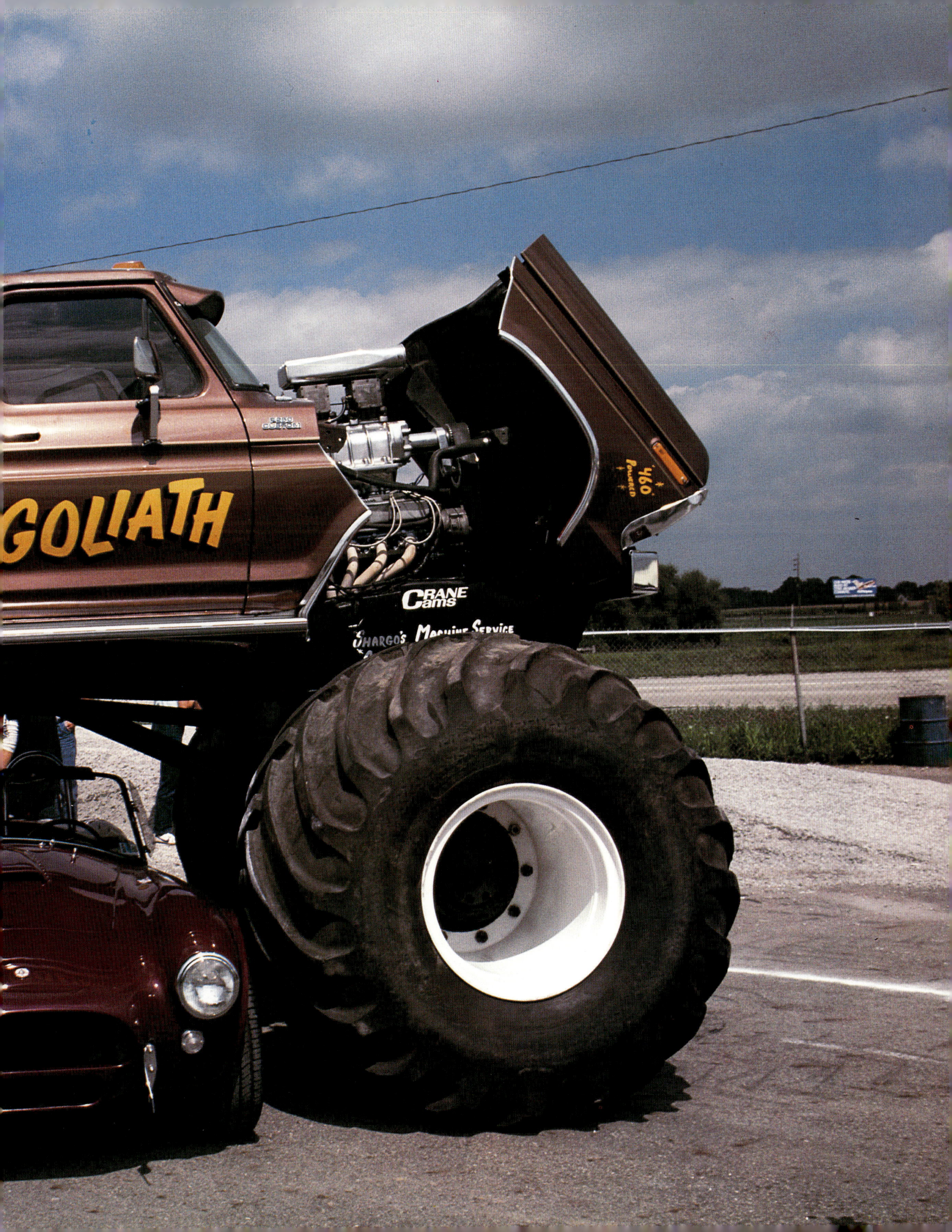
GOLIATH
460 POWERED
CRANE Cams
Shargo's Machine Service

ACES HIGH

KING KONG

Monster Trucks Illustrated 77

SHOWTIME

THE TEXAS TOY

GRAVE DIGGER

Monster Truck Log

LON-RANGER
Gary Bauer — Vienna, Ohio

SONS OF THUNDER II
Milton Bell — Minneapolis, MN

KODIAK
Mark Bendler — Milwaukee, WI

E'VIL
Mark Berger — Beltsville, MD

LITTLE FOOT
Charlie Brown — Glendale, AZ

BLACK KNIGHT
Michael Brady — Glendale, AZ

THE ENFORCER
Mark & Holly Chapman
West Granby, Ct

BLUE THUNDER
Kevin Dabney — Fayetteville, NC

THUMPER
Earl Dagit — Holiday, FL

SKOAL BANDIT
Seth Doulton — Santa Barbara, CA

MICHIGAN ICE MONSTER
Brett Engelman — Grand Rapids, MI

TRUK
Darrell Eve — Bozeman, MT

LED BUTTERFLY
Tom Feeny — Portland, OR

OUTLAW 35
Kenny Fewox — Polk City, FL

HOG MACHINE
Charles F. Flynn — Henagar, AL

FIRST BLOOD
Rob Fuchs — Woodstock, IL

CYCLOPS
Gary Cardiner — Bakersfield, CA

GIGANTIC ORANGE CRUST
Joe Gardner — Freckenridge, MO

BARBARIAN
Bruce Gault — San Jose, CA

INTIMIDATOR
Tim Greenfield — Dubuque, IA

KRIMSON KRUSHER
Dale Hancock — Evansville, IN

USA I
Everett Jasmer — Springlake, MN

TINY TANK
Andy Kotuby — Ellwood City, PA

SAMSON I
Don Maples — Huntsville, AL

EXCALIBUR
Dave Marquart — Maumee, OH

RENEGADE I
Greg Martin — Mountain Home, AR

BARBARIAN
Bob & Jim Miller — Nokomis, IL

MASTERS OF DISASTER
Mrgs Enterprises — Albany, MN

ROLLIN' THUNDER
Jim Oldaker — Redondo Beach, CA

LONE EAGLE
Allen Pezo — Millington, MI

BEARFOOT
Fred Shafer — Granite City, IL

SHOWTIME
Brian Shell — Fraser, MI

CRIMSON GIANT
Marvin & Jean Smith — Arnold, MO

ALTITUDE PLUS
Ed Socie — Fullerton, CA

LIL' ALL AMERICAN, THE EAGLE & THE ALL AMERICAN
Spikers' All American 4x4 —
Lakeland, FL

FRANKENSTEIN & MONSTER VETTE
Cliff Starbird — Ivane KS

KING KRUNCH & KING KRUNCH II
Scott Stephens — Woodlands, TX

GODZILLA
Alvin Thurber — Pawtucket, RI

VIRGINIA BEACH BEAST
William Townes — Norfolk, VA

HEAVY METAL
Mike Trinagle — Bronx, NY

GOLIATH
Alan Tura — Warren, OH

HERCULES
Larry Tura — Clairton, PA

BRUTTE BOSS HOG
Randy Weber — Bristol, IN

MONSTER MASH & DESTROYER I
Mike Welch — Berlingham, WA

THE GUARDIAN
Dean Wilfur — Dawson Creek, BC

CAJUN KING
Mart Williams — Sulphur, LA

TAURUS
Jack Willman — Madison, IL

VIRGINIA GIANT
Diehl Wilson — Winchester, VA

PAC MAN
Roccy Giles — Goose Creek, SC

HERCULES
Scott Hess — Auburn, IN

SOUTHERN NIGHTMARE
Ricky Green — Myrtle Beach, SC

MR. TWISTER
Dave Stazak — Wausau, WI

KING OF THE ROAD
Don Buckholtz — Wyoming, Iowa

AWESOME KONG
Jeff Dane — Colene, TX

GENTLE BEN
Kevin Preswell — Greenwood, IN

PONY EXPRESS
Tommy Bryant — Pennsacola, FL

TERMINATOR II
Denny/Bud Maerkisch
Norwalk, OH

BIG TOW
Ray Piorkowski — Florissant, MO

SAN DIEGAN
Gary Schott — San Marcos, CA

BIGFOOT (A registered trademark of Bigfoot 4x4)
Bob Chandler — St Louis, MO

...AND MANY MORE !!!